THE COMPLETE S. P9-CBQ-449 **MANY WOMEN NEVER HAVE...**
YOU CAN NOW MAKE POSSIBLE
FOR YOURSELF

FOR YOURSELF is a unique book on female
sexuality. First, because it's written by a
woman therapist who's been highly successful in
helping women achieve more sexual pleasure.
Second, because respect for women and warm
understanding mark every page. And finally,
because it offers honesty, scientific clarity,
and detailed exercises.

FOR YOURSELF is based on a refreshing
premise. Psychologist Lonnie Barbach urges you
to enjoy your sexual potential to the fullest—
not to satisfy a partner, *not* to fulfill some
psychological ideal of normality, but *for yourself*.
Only now are we learning how women *really*
experience sex. Our beliefs used to come from
men writing about *women's* feelings, so if
we didn't personally experience what we read,
we'd feel inadequate, not quite normal.

FOR YOURSELF brings together the latest
scientific facts on female sexual response with a
program of unusual techniques that you can
practice by yourself to achieve greater sexual
satisfaction and orgasmic pleasure.
*Here are facts and insights that you
won't find anywhere else.*

FOR YOURSELF
The Fulfillment of Female Sexuality

For Yourself:
The Fulfillment
of
Female Sexuality

Lonnie Garfield Barbach

A SIGNET BOOK

NEW AMERICAN LIBRARY

*This book is dedicated
to all women who want to develop
their sexual and nonsexual potential*

SIGNET TRADEMARK REG. U.S. PAT. OFF. AND FOREIGN COUNTRIES
REGISTERED TRADEMARK—MARCA REGISTRADA
HECHO EN CHICAGO, U.S.A.

SIGNET, SIGNET CLASSIC, MENTOR, PLUME, MERIDIAN AND NAL
BOOKS *are published by New American Library,
1633 Broadway, New York, New York 10019*

FIRST SIGNET PRINTING, MAY, 1976

14   15   16   17   18   19

PRINTED IN THE UNITED STATES OF AMERICA

CONTENTS

ACKNOWLEDGMENTS

My most sincere thanks to my secretary Dianne Cooper, who interpreted my hieroglyphics, to my editor, Kate Medina, who translated them into English, to Dr. Bernie Zilbergeld, Karen Jacobs, and especially Dr. Jay Mann, who devoted time and energy to reading the manuscript, and to Drummond Pike for seeing the process through. I could not have written the book without their help.

I would also like to thank Nancy Carlsen, B. K. Moran, Rebecca Black, Dr. Lynnette Beall, Mary Anne Ver Steege, Toni Ayres, Maggi Rubenstein, June Stanbaugh, Carolyn Smith, Myesha Jenkins, Chuck Jenkins, Marlene Braverman, and my other friends and colleagues who contributed information and perspective. And Betty Dodson for the illustration.

Special thanks and appreciation to the women in the groups who shared their intimate thoughts and feelings and gave me much of the information on which this book is based.

INTRODUCTION

So you've never had an orgasm, or you don't think you have. Or perhaps you only have had orgasms occasionally, or solely through self-stimulation and not with a partner. Or, perhaps you just wish you knew more about female sexuality and orgasm.

Do you sometimes feel that you would be happier if sex were eliminated from your intimate relationships altogether? If so, possibly you feel abnormal in this regard, or like a misfit or not whole as a woman. Or, perhaps you just feel that you are missing something everyone else has enjoyed, a part of life that you'd like to have be a part of yours too. You probably feel as if you are one of only a few women who have this problem. The truth is that you are far from alone.

In the course of my work as a psychologist and sex therapist with the University of California Medical Center in San Francisco, I have become acutely aware of the extent of the problem many women have in understanding their sexual natures, and in reaching orgasm. Recent statistics on sexual behavior bear out my impressions. In the 1970s the Playboy Foundation sponsored a study of the sexual behavior of 1044 females;[1] in this study, professional sex therapists repeated the kind of study Kinsey made on 5940 females in the 1940s.[2] The results of the 1972 study, some of which have been included by Morton Hunt in his book *Sexual Behavior In The 1970's*, indicate that despite the so-called sexual revolution, not much progress has been made in orgasmic responsivity among females.

Both the Kinsey study and the 1972 study indicate that only about half the married women in the United States experience orgasm with any consistency in their sexual relationships. In 1972, 53 per cent[3]—only about half—of the women (married an average of fifteen years) achieved orgasm with intercourse 90 to 100 per cent of the time, while in the

1938–49 study the figure was 45 per cent.[4] The 1972 report also shows that only 30 per cent[5] of the single women interviewed were consistently orgasmic with a partner; and that approximately 15 per cent[6] of the women never or almost never experienced orgasm.

Traditional psychotherapy views the presence of a sexual problem as a symptom of an underlying psychological problem or "neurosis." Books such as David Reuben's *Everything You Always Wanted to Know About Sex* foster the notion that "the only effective treatment for total orgasmic impairment is psychotherapy, because the condition is a psychiatric one. The sexual difficulty is simply a manifestation of a deeper emotional dysfunction."[7] As a result of this perspective, many women have been needlessly worried and have paid large sums of money to psychiatrists, and even so experience little or no change in sexual responsivity.

In recent years, Dr. William Masters and Virginia Johnson, developed a treatment program specifically designed for couples experiencing sexual difficulties. At the University of California Student Health Service in Berkeley, I worked as a therapist treating couples according to the basic Masters and Johnson technique. In this form of therapy, a woman who is not orgasmic is given treatment with her male partner.

Gradually, however, we began to realize that not only was couple treatment too expensive for many women, but also by its very nature it was unavailable to many people who needed help; it restricted treatment to only those women who had steady sexual partners, and to those women whose steady partners were willing and able to attend the counseling sessions. This meant that a large number of women who wanted and needed help were excluded—women whose partners were unwilling or unable to participate in formal treatment, families aho could not afford costly couple treatment, women who did not have a steady partner with whom to attend couple treatment, women in homosexual relationships, or the many women who for various private reasons did not want to involve their partners, at first, in the problem.

And so, in order to provide help for more women, regardless of the nature of their intimate relationships, I developed, with Nancy Carlsen, a new kind of group treatment program for women which did not entail working directly with a partner[8]—although a more satisfying sexual relationship with a partner remained a primary goal for most women. The new treatment program borrowed elements from the Masters and Johnson therapy technique,[9] and also from other established sex therapy programs, including the series of exercises developed in 1971 by Drs. Lobitz and LoPiccolo at the University of Oregon.[10] What is distinctive about the program is that we worked with women only, in a group situation, and combined a number of therapeutic techniques.

We called the groups "pre-orgasmic" women's groups. Pre-orgasmic seemed a more appropriate term than non-orgasmic since we fully expected that a woman who entered the group would be orgasmic before the program ended. Each group met for ten sessions of one hour and a half each, spaced over a period of five weeks. Two female co-leaders ran the groups. There were five to seven women in each group who were strangers to each other before the first meeting.

The women ranged in age from eighteen to fifty-eight years old and came from a variety of ethnic, racial, regional, and religious backgrounds—although as it happens, the majority of the women were Caucasian and American born. Some were married, some single, others divorced or separated. Some were students, some housewives, some professionals, and others were unskilled workers—although the majority were from what might be generally termed the middle class. A few women were in homosexual relationships, but most were in heterosexual relationships and the language of the book reflects this bias. I believe that most of the concepts and techniques in the forthcoming chapters can be helpful to a majority of women. However, each woman is unique—the nature of her relationships, her personality, her background, and her physiological responsivity color her approach to sex as well as to other aspects of her life. In light of this, a considerable variety of exercises are presented, along with discussion of some common difficulties and obstacles encountered by many of the women with whom I have worked.

In a sense the women who participated in the first group sessions are the real authors of this book. When I started the group treatment program, I was already an experienced sex therapist, but the groups taught me a great deal. I want to thank these women (whose names I have changed in the book to protect their privacy) for sharing their lives in the kind of candid detail that enables me to pass on to you not only information, but also specific examples of real life situations and problems. I hope their candor helps you to open your own experience so that it satisfies your personal needs and desires more fully. In the words of one group member, Carmen, "I hope very strongly that other women will benefit from this therapy as I did. There is a stage where you cannot hope any longer to manage alone, by yourself. I was there and a lot of women must be there too. I hope that they can find their way to this kind of treatment."

In the group meetings the women shared stories about their sexual difficulties and confusions, their personal feelings about their sexual problems. Each woman gained insights into her own difficulties from the shared experiences; and each one gained support from the other women's reflections on the possible sources of their sexual difficulties.

In addition to attending the group sessions, each woman was expected to do one hour of homework every day. This homework, an adaptation of the nine-step masturbation program of LoPiccolo,[11] is fully outlined in this book. The first homework assignments are directed toward helping the woman get in touch with her own body and sexual feelings. Later in the program, when the woman is comfortably orgasmic through self-stimulation, the partner's participation is included in the homework—and so it is included in this book, even though the partner never participates directly in the formal group process.

The treatment, then, is a combination of group discussions, physiological information about female anatomy and female sexuality, homework exercises, and individualized instruction. The women returned to the group twice a week with new ideas and stories of progress. They worked together and helped each other. They worked hard; they cried, they laughed, they fumed with anger. But most importantly they did the exercises that paved the way for fuller orgasmic sexual response.

Since the first group met in November 1972, several hundred women have participated in this type of treatment with phenomenal success. Statistics compiled by the Human Sexuality Program at the University of California Medical Center indicate that 93 per cent of the women who entered the program, many of whom had never experienced an orgasm, left five weeks later experiencing orgasm consistently, usually through self-stimulation. Of course, the five-week program could not completely reverse a problem, especially if a woman had experienced it for years. The treatment is based on the premise that the woman will continue the exercises on her own, at home. Generally, within three months after the group sessions were over, more than half the women could experience orgasm with partners. After eight months, the percentage was even higher.

Statistics are still being compiled, but the experiences of a pilot group of seventeen women who were closely followed for eight months following program participation appear typical. Twelve were consistently orgasmic with a partner while three others were orgasmic over 25 per cent of the time with a partner. Most, but not all, of the women who reported orgasms with a partner experienced them during coitus. Some experienced them through other forms of love play.

I continue to maintain contact with the women who participated in the groups in case new problems might arise as the result of the changes which allowed them to experience orgasm. To date, no serious or lasting problems have been reported.

But achieving orgasm was only part of the change that occurred. Frequently, the impact of the program positively changed the women's attitudes and feelings about themselves. By getting in touch with themselves sexually, the women gradually became more comfortable with their own bodies, more sure of themselves. Betty summed up the change in her feelings about her physical self this way: "I feel very confident now about my own body's ability to perform. I have learned to admire my body and to enjoy it." The simple act of taking the time each day from a busy schedule to do the homework exercises, making more time for themselves and their needs, helped many of the women realize that they deserved more for themselves, and consequently further increased their feelings of self-worth. Many of them began to realize that other people were willing to respond positively to their requests for change. Before their experience in the group, many of the women just assumed that their requests for change would be rejected or ignored, and so never attempted even to begin asking.

Another important outcome of the program was that the women began to take responsibility for their own sexuality; taking more initiative, communicating their likes and dislikes more actively. This is essential to becoming orgasmic, and this assumption of responsibility also seems to spread to other areas of a woman's life. Recent research by Arvalea Nelson indicates that consistently orgasmic women tend to describe themselves as contented, good-natured, insightful, self-confident, independent, realistic, strong, capable, and understanding while non-orgasmic women tend to describe themselves as bitter, despondent, dissatisfied, distrustful, fussy, immature, inhibited, prejudiced, and sulky.[12]

My aim in writing this book is to share what has been learned about female sexuality from the groups at the University of California Medical Center. My hope is that the book will serve some of the same functions that the group and orgasmic treatment did for the women who participated in it. The information is also pertinent for men and women without orgasmic difficulties, who want to extend their sexual awareness, and for male and female therapists and educators. In the book I will address the female reader directly. I have tried to provide the physiological information, the psychological support and the exercises to enable you to learn more about your own body and its needs, to realize your own sexual potential and also to overcome the sexual difficulties you may have.

Since the most frequent complaint from women who are dissatisfied with their sex lives is lack of orgasms, this book is specifically designed to counteract that problem. However, since orgasm is just one enjoyable aspect of sex, the larger purpose of the book is to give the reader information, permission, and support to enable her to experiment and obtain greater satisfaction and enjoyment out of sex whether or not orgasm occurs.

Although sex is one important aspect, much more than sex is involved in a loving relationship. Learning to be open, to share, to communicate, and be intimate in non-sexual ways also takes learning and practice. Since some of the non-sexual relationship aspects are beyond the scope of this book, I suggest as additional reading George Bach's books *Pairing* and *The Intimate Enemy*, Pierre Mornell's *The Lovebook*, and *Becoming Partners* by Carl Rogers.

The book's structure will follow the general structure of the group therapy program. By reading about the situations, feelings, and experiences of other women, you may be reassured and given a clearer perspective on your own situation. All of us are comforted by knowing that we are not the only person with certain feelings or difficulties. Misinformation about women's sexuality is prevalent, and I hope to replace some of it with more accurate information. In addition to basic information about female sexuality, and stories from the groups, much of the material in the book is aimed at helping you understand your own body and your own sexual responses. Listening closely to the women in the groups destroyed any lingering belief I may have had that there is one way, or a right way, for a woman to respond sexually. Listening carefully to the women changed some of my own attitudes about traditional love-making and called into question some of the stereotypes under which I had unwittingly been operating. Possibly you'll discover the same for yourself. Each woman is unique. Although women have some sexual likes, dislikes, and responses in common, basically each woman has an idiosyncratic sexual pattern that is all her own.[13] Just as each of us knows what diet works best when we want to lose weight, and what will best cheer us up when we are feeling blue, each woman can know her sexual self and be an authority on her own body. Once you understand yourself better, it's easier to communicate your sexual needs to a partner.

It may be necessary to reread certain sections of the book from time to time, and to practice the exercises a number of times before they become effective; the women in the groups frequently found this necessary. Some of the suggestions and exercises might at first seem startling or extreme, but experience has shown that they work.

Since there is no right or wrong, normal or abnormal way to be sexually stimulated, the book makes no attempt to fit you into a mold. Rather its purpose is to encourage you to explore yourself in order to discover your unique sexual responses, at your own speed and with your own goals in mind. My purpose in the book is to provide information that may help you, and in turn help you advise a daughter or friend.

One of the women in the group, the wife of a minister, confided to me that she had approached the group with trepidation, fearing that her religious beliefs might be questioned or faintly ridiculed by the group, or held responsible for her sexual difficulties. After the group was over she was delighted to find that her sexual problem had been almost fully solved without challenge at all to her religious orientation. Without question it is possible to change your orgasmic response without changing your whole value system—although some of the more traditional views of what is sometimes considered "normal" sexuality may be called into question.

In order to help you begin to understand your individual responsiveness, the exercises begin with self-sexuality. Our group discussions revealed that it is essential for a woman to get in touch with her own body and understand her individual requirements for orgasm before she can effectively communicate her needs to a partner. The easiest and most effective means of getting in touch with one's sexual responses is through masturbation. Although important in itself, masturbation turns out to be a very important stepping stone to a healthier, happier self, and a more satisfying and fulfilling sexual relationship with a partner.

1: Sex and Orgasm

Did you know that minor surgery can be performed on the inner two thirds of the vagina without an anesthetic?[1] Did you know that orgasms with masturbation are usually subjectively reported and objectively recorded as more intense than those resulting from coitus?[2] Did you know that a number of women experience orgasms without even knowing they are doing so?

Because of the fairly widespread ignorance about female sexuality, orgasm is a concern of many, if not most, women. Since we have grown up in a society which, until recently, prohibited much open and direct discussion of sex, many women were left feeling that their own sexual problems or discomforts were unique. When I first met Betty, she had never had an orgasm and had no idea how to go about achieving one. She felt as if there must be a sort of secret, magical society to which some women somehow belonged, and membership qualified those women to have orgasms; that somehow she had never found out how to become a member of the club. It is easy to understand why Betty felt this way; she could think of no other explanation for why she was not privileged to experience orgasm as other women were.

Until recently, it really was not known exactly what women experienced sexually. Most of what was believed came from writings by men about women's experiences. If what was described in the sex manuals did not match a woman's own personal experiences, she assumed they described the experience of most other women. And the mythical experiences described in such books made many women feel inadequate, abnormal. A woman may have secretly hoped that her responses would some day match up with those detailed in the books. The fact that friends rarely discussed sexual problems frankly only confirmed a woman's fears that she was one of the few people having any difficulty in this area. There

17

was almost no information on the subject from a woman's point of view.

In recent years, through more open communication, and with increased scientific investigations into female sexuality, some solid information has been gathered, and these findings describe the sexual experiences of women more accurately than the old sexual myths used to. Basically, the findings show that most women *do* have trouble having orgasm with intercourse.

The statistics cited in the Introduction which show that approximately half of the sexual encounters that end in orgasm for a male partner do not end in orgasm for a female partner give us something to wonder about. If women are not sexually dysfunctional for biological reasons (and how could so many of them be?) it must mean that the current sexual practices employed by many couples, while meeting the needs of a large majority of men, do not meet the unique needs of women. I think it's fair to assume that scientifically, women have the same biological need and capacity for orgasm as men, and that with individual exploration, couple communication, and valid sexual information, women can become capable of enjoying sex and responding orgasmically as often as they wish.

Why all the fuss about orgasm? Why is it so important and why does the absence of orgasm cause so much frustration and concern? Orgasm is a very pleasurable feeling. More importantly, orgasm is the natural and normal release of sexual tension. Sexual tension builds up in women just as it does in men. It builds up not only as the result of sexual encounters, but as the result of normal daily activities; the things we see, hear, touch, and think. It builds up more or less depending upon the individual woman and the experiences of her day. And in many women, this build-up of tension requires a release which is just as natural a process as the build-up itself. In some women, tension may dissipate without orgasm, while in other women, a continual, repeated lack of sexual release can cause irritability, frustration, fatigue or even headaches. Stress resulting from sexual or other problems can create body imbalances which may result in vaginal infections and other physical symptoms and gynecological problems.[3] With an orgasmic release, pleasure, relaxation, a feeling of well-being usually result.

Perhaps the best way to describe it would be in the words

of Lydia, who wrote after she began to experience orgasm for the first time: "The atmosphere has to be warm, comfortable. No harsh sounds. Feeling of delicious warmth all over skin, like covered with warm velvet. Then I begin to concentrate on increasingly pleasant sensations. I feel like I have something extremely warm and soft in my mouth. Sensations more and more strong and pleasurable in clitoral area and begin radiating from there to all parts of me. My heart pounds like crazy. I only breathe when I have to. Every part of me seems to extend from my clitoris: head, throat, feet. Then it happens—deep, warm waves roll over and through me in a beautiful rhythm. I always think 'this is the best *ever*.' And then it stops. I'd like to get past the comparison so it would last forever."

That is a description of what one experience of orgasm was like for one woman. Other women report different experiences, each as unique as the woman herself.

Orgasm, then, is a natural, normal, healthy process. No woman should be prohibited from enjoying the joy of sexual release in her own individual way. It can be as important and necessary for a woman to enjoy sex as it is for her to enjoy her work, children, environment, food, or recreational activities. It's just another potentially satisfying aspect of life.

A woman should be able to enjoy sex not only because her body is designed for sexual enjoyment, but because a satisfying sexual relationship helps to create a closer and more fulfilling emotional relationship with another person—a lover in the best sense.

Sex has been, and continues to be, a serious point of contention in many relationships. A woman's failure to respond orgasmically within the sexual relationship frequently becomes a source of conflict for the couple,[4] either directly or indirectly, and it is often difficult for a woman to maintain an enthusiastic attitude toward sex if she is not achieving orgasm most of the time. Clark and Wallin reported that two thirds of the women who had orgasms all or most of the time enjoyed marital intercourse very much, whereas only one sixth of those who rarely or never had orgasms did.[5]

A pre-orgasmic woman may come to resent her husband or lover's sexual advances and develop ways to avoid them whenever possible. This in turn can have a stifling effect on her partner's demonstrations of affection, not only in the sexual area, but in other areas of intimacy as well. These unexpressed emotions often emerge—the result of some incident, sexual or otherwise—as destructive forces in the relationship. In most cases, if a close relationship is to continue and grow, sex must be a rewarding experience for both people involved.

Then, too, why should a woman leave a sexual encounter feeling frustrated and angry, sad and disappointed, when open relaxed love-making, which often concludes in orgasm, can be such a joyous and validating experience? Laurie describes her feelings after orgasm as being, "like a wave has washed over me leaving me spent and so relaxed I want to turn over and go to sleep . . . a tranquilizer. I want to cuddle up to my husband and rest. Often I will have two or three orgasms. Psychologically this is a real boost. It makes me feel important and very good about myself." Sex and orgasm, then, are normal human functions, and vital parts of a loving relationship. Moreover, sexual responsiveness is an important part of a woman's self-image. Most of the women I have worked with felt that there must be something basically wrong with them because they did not have orgasms. The women felt vaguely ashamed of themselves, and tried to hide the problem from others—either by not talking about it, or by keeping sexual encounters to a minimum and faking orgasm when they did make love. Connie claimed that her husband separated from her as a result of her sexual unresponsiveness. At the time she entered the group, she had had no sexual relationships since their separation. Because she had never had an orgasm, she felt incomplete as a woman and could not imagine that another man would want her, given this inability. So feeling good about oneself and one's responsivity as a female can be another important reason to have orgasms.

A number of common fears, false expectations, and misinformation seem to prevent many women from realizing their full sexual potential.

The first erroneous belief shared by many women in the therapy program is that sexual behavior comes naturally. A colleague of mine, Thea Lowry, puts it well, "Although sex is perfectly natural, it is not always naturally perfect." Many women don't know how to respond orgasmically and yet they feel they *should* know, just naturally, since sex is supposed to be a normal animal instinct. So there is a tendency to just wait for it to "happen," for something to click. Unsatisfactory sex comes naturally, but good sex, for both men and women, requires information, practice, communication, and co-operation. Women are not "frigid." The term "frigid" implies numerous negative psychological attributes.

The human brain is the most complex of any species. According to Ford and Beach, "This explains why, in human beings more than other species, sexuality is structured and patterned by learning."[6] Sex is less instinctive in the human being. Like any other skill, it needs to be learned and to be practiced. Kinsey found that as the years of marital sexual experience increased, sexual responsivity increased.[7] Margaret Mead found that in the human female the potentiality for orgasm is a cultural factor. If a society considers orgasmic release of the female important, then the essential love-making techniques which ensure the woman's orgasm will be learned and practiced. If the female orgasm is considered unimportant, the members of the culture will not practice techniques essential to orgasmic release in the woman; and women are likely to be anorgasmic.[8]

A second erroneous expectation is that the man should be the authority on sex—that the man is responsible for the woman's orgasm. Expecting this to be the case can lead to all sorts of erroneous conclusions. "Maybe it's not love," is one way of dismissing the difficulty. After all, you might feel that if it were really love, you would feel so turned on that you would naturally have orgasms. Because you don't have orgasms, you may assume that your partner must not be "Mr. Right," and you must not really be "in love" with him. Besides, if he really loved you, wouldn't he know how to "give" you an orgasm? Since he doesn't give you orgasms, you may conclude that he must not love you enough.

These feelings stem from the misconception that the man should know all there is to know about sex. After all, isn't a woman trained to be innocent until married, when her husband is then supposed to teach her the things she needs to know about sex? Most of us have never been given much accurate and specific information about sex, but rather have been led to believe that sex is a man's area of expertise. And if a woman is experienced, she is taught that she should remain silent about it. As I think back on it now, I grew up believing men were somehow born with the knowledge about sex, never thinking that they, too, needed to be taught just as I did. Dr. Bernie Zilbergeld, a colleague who leads sex therapy groups for men, reports that many of the men in his program say they would love it if their partners were free in expressing sexual desires. The men felt this would relieve them of a heavy burden—they could admit some sexual ignorance and stop straining to seem expert.

Men do not have any magical answers for successful sex and they are not capable of reading a woman's mind to find out what she wants and needs. They need to learn how a woman likes to make love, just as they need to learn how she takes her coffee. Waiting for "Mr. Right" to come along and light your orgasmic fire could take forever. One might go from lover to lover in search of the explosive spark, failing to work on the positive possibilities of any one relationship. Women who have had many lovers expect their solution to come when they find a truly meaningful relationship, while women who are involved in a rewarding and intimate relationship, but have few or no other lovers, secretly suspect that the answer lies in experiencing a variety of men.

Sally and Rita were in the same women's group. Rita reported more than fifty different male sex partners and claimed that if only she could find a meaningful and long-term relationship, her orgasmic problem would be solved. Sally, on the other hand, was a virgin when she married, and continued to be very much in love with her husband. She secretly suspected, however, that if she had just had more experience with other lovers, her problem would be over. They each realized, hearing the other talk, that the solution didn't necessarily lie in the number of different lovers, or the intensity of the relationship. Women in intense relationships can be non-orgasmic while others in casual affairs might have little or no difficulty achieving orgasm.

Sometimes looking for the right man is translated into the search for the "magic penis." If you could just find the right penis—a bigger one, a smaller one—or if you could just find an erection that would last long enough, your orgasmic problems would be solved. But the fact is that the size of an erect penis varies only slightly.[9] Moreover, intercourse is only one technique for love-making; women can reach orgasm through other kinds of stimulation—oral or manual. So the male partner doesn't even have to have an erection at all to satisfy a woman sexually. The kind of stimulation that suits the specific woman is what counts. This is especially important because no two women respond in exactly the same way sexually. Each individual has her own personal likes, dislikes, and favorite types of stimulation. But, of course, a woman can't tell a partner what she likes, what stimulates her best, if she doesn't know herself. Basically, an understanding of your unique sexual self, sometimes most easily acquired by the process of self-stimulation, can put you in a better position to help your partner learn how to please you.

Another false expectation is that orgasm "should" occur through intercourse alone; women tend to feel sexually "immature," even "neurotic" if they require direct clitoral stimulation to achieve orgasm. They disqualify these orgasms. They want "vaginal" orgasms. They want orgasms the "right" way—that is, during intercourse. We have bought the idea that the vagina is the primary sex organ and that therefore, the only real way to have a "mature" orgasm is through the thrusting of the penis in and out of the vagina.

In reality, the clitoris is the female sex organ. Roughly comparable in sensitivity to the penis, the clitoris serves no other function than that of providing sexual pleasure. The vagina is comparable in sensitivity to the male testicles. Therefore, if instead of sexual intercourse, which directly stimulates the male's most sensitive organ, and only indirectly stimulates the female's most sexually sensitive organ, love-making were practiced by a male rubbing the clitoris with his testicles—then women would be orgasmic and men would be in groups of pre-orgasmic treatment!

As Sarah put it when she first came to the group, "If the old thrusting in and out would do it, it would have happened by now. Since it didn't, I'm now ready to try other things." The physiological fact is that intercourse alone just doesn't seem to provide enough of the right kind of stimulation in the right area to permit many women to become aroused to the point of orgasm. Physiologically, it may not be possible for you to have orgasms through intercourse unless you also receive additional direct clitoral stimulation. As Ann Koedt says, "if certain sexual positions now defined as 'standard' are not mutually conducive to orgasm, they must no longer be defined as standard."[10]

Another common erroneous expectation is that a woman should have her orgasm at the same time her partner does, in one glorious simultaneous climax. I'm certain none of these "shoulds" have been scripted by women. They just don't meet many physiological requirements for female orgasm.

One of the most detrimental of the erroneous beliefs is that sex is not as necessary for women as it is for men. Women are taught that a woman does not need the sexual release that a man does, that a man's sexual needs are greater than a woman's and she must accommodate to his needs. This can produce an unfortunate situation at either extreme. If a woman feels she has no rights of her own, but must accommodate her partner whenever he is sexually interested, she will very likely end up feeling resentful most of the time. Constant sexual availability is not part of the marriage vows. On the other hand, if a woman believes she is not supposed to express herself sexually, she may inhibit her natural desire for fear she will appear unfeminine.

Woman is not asexual. If she is aggressive and assertive sexually it doesn't mean she is masculine. Passivity is not the normal female state. Expressing yourself sexually for yourself and not just for your partner is important.

Feelings of repulsion and disgust about sex can be a factor inhibiting sexual expression. Sex repulsion is a reaction usually based on early negative messages about sex, some of which may have been perceived unconsciously. The most prevalent basis for repulsion toward sex comes from the erroneous idea that women's genitals are disgusting and unclean and hence sex is disgusting and unclean. As children, our genitals became associated with the organs of excretion and we grew up feeling that "down there" was an unclean and unacceptable part of our body. Lydia never had an orgasm. She never touched her genitals directly with her hands because she felt her genitals were so repulsive. She found great difficulty in even looking at the area in a mirror, but after doing so was surprised that it was much nicer than she had anticipated. She overcame her negative feelings about her genitals by getting more familiar with them, both visually and tactilely, and soon thereafter could experience orgasms with masturbation. Eve always felt her vagina was extremely dirty and was surprised to learn that the vagina is generally cleaner than the mouth.

Other reasons for developing a repulsion toward sex can come from experiences of sexual contact with adults at an early age—rape and other incidents that may cause a young woman to feel dirty, promiscuous, or repulsive because of the expression of her sexuality. As a child Eve had been sexually fondled by her father and her older brother. Her brother, in particular, threatened to physically hurt her if she refused to submit or if she told anyone about it. Quite understandably, she could not reconcile the pleasurable sexual feelings with the fact that she was doing something that was considered wrong by others. When she grew older and married, any sexual feeling brought up the old feelings associated with her childhood sexual experiences, feelings she had spent years trying to forget. It was difficult for Eve to explore her sexuality because she really would have preferred to experience no sexual feelings whatsoever. This sort of experience is surprisingly common. An educated guess places incest at about one million cases per year in the United States.[11] The 1972 Playboy Foundation Study found that 9.2 per cent of the females interviewed had had some sexual contact with a relative.[12] Old traumas don't die quickly, but gradually Eve is becoming more comfortable with experiencing and expressing her sexual feelings as an adult who has some control in her adult sexual relationship.

Another source of inhibition is the fear some women have that they will look ugly while they are having an orgasm and that their partners will be repulsed and find them unattractive. This was a tremendous fear of Carmen's and after her partner saw her having an orgasm for the first time she repeatedly asked him if she looked ugly, if he was repulsed, and if he still loved her. He responded very supportively and told her that she looked beautiful and that he loved her. After having a few more orgasms and still no negative remarks, she was finally convinced he was telling the truth.

The fear of losing control, of fainting, or of screaming while having an orgasm is another common fear among women who have never experienced orgasm. All the Victorian pornographic novels depict women as fainting or dying away when they have an orgasm. This does not happen in reality. However, the fear of losing consciousness is only natural since at the point of orgasm, there is lessened outside awareness. Carmen became very upset because, as she was about to experience her first orgasm with masturbation, her lover touched her. She had not even been aware that he had entered the room and had neither heard nor seen him because she was so involved in self-stimulation. This intense sexual involvement really distressed her. However, the fact that she regained control when he touched her helped her to realize that she hadn't lost consciousness, but just that she had her attention focused more internally than externally.

Carmen was able to overcome this experience and have her first orgasm a few days later.

Carol was afraid she would have to grow up and become a responsible woman if she had orgasms. Eve felt that going "all the way" meant having an orgasm and rationalized that she was really a "good girl" because even though she was having sex, in her terms she was not "going all the way." She could let her sexual feelings go only so far—even though she was married. Leslie was afraid she would do things she thoght were immoral if she started experiencing orgasms. Other women, including Janice, were afraid that having an orgasm would change their lives. What did happen when these women began having orgasms after the therapy program? Carol didn't have to grow up any more than she wanted to. Eve was no less virtuous and certainly never became promiscuous. Leslie became a little less conservative, but definitely not immoral or perverted by her standards, and Janice's whole life didn't change. She just felt a little bit better about herself and a whole lot better about sex.

Many things cause changes in our lives. Few of us live by a totally regimented routine that never varies. We marry, divorce, have children, our children get older and finally leave home, we change jobs, we move to a new house, and unexpected events cause us to change our plans. But we usually have some measure of control over our life circumstances. A tornado of change doesn't usually uproot us and whirl us around to the degree that we don't recognize our former selves. Changes are generally slow and gradual.

Experiencing orgasms when you haven't previously might result in greater enjoyment of sex, a closer, more intimate relationship, and possibly even less sexual inhibitions and greater assertiveness in the sexual area. You might note some of these changes, but I doubt that you'll feel so different that you won't recognize yourself or that all your life problems will suddenly appear resolved.

Some women fear that if they become orgasmic with a man that they will be completely dependent upon him and hence more vulnerable. Evelyn never felt she could trust men. She said men could never be counted on; that they will just take off and leave you. She feared that if she became orgasmic with her husband, she would be more vulnerable if he left her because then she would be dependent upon him for orgasms. Objectively this just doesn't make sense, even though the fear is real. If you can have orgasms with one partner, you can probably have them with another or by yourself through masturbation. No one "gives" you orgasms. You are the one in control. You let them happen or shut them off. Furthermore, it's likely you'll be just as vulnerable and hurt if your lover left you whether or not you had been having orgasms when you made love.

A real fear that can keep some women from doing anything to solve their sexual problems is the fear of failure. When Harriet joined the group she didn't think she could really become orgasmic. She said, "If I tried, I'd only fail, and then I'd be *really* miserable." Harriet felt hopeless and helpless. She had created a self-fulfilling prophecy. By deciding ahead of time that she would fail, she never really tried to do anything positive to become orgasmic. The group members pointed out that if she *never* tried to do anything about it her prophecy *would* come true. She would never become orgasmic. However, if she tried—conscientiously—she would at least have a chance to succeed.

Harriet eventually did defy her fears, as did all the other women mentioned. It takes time and effort to counteract these fears. It means saying "I'm afraid" and yet pushing beyond.

All of the sexual fears, myths, erroneous expectations I have described were first mentioned by the pre-orgasmic women with whom I have worked. You may have some of these same fears or, perhaps, different ones. The women in the groups started having orgasms despite their fears, and you can too; or, if you already are orgasmic but not consistently, you can build a richer sexual life.

Are any of the points that have been discussed true for you? Are you pre-orgasmic because you're different and hence special if you don't have orgasms? Do you feel that you have been so deprived in your past that it's too late, that you can't make up for all your early deprivations now? It's never too late. Many women begin enjoying sex more as they grow older. Leslie was forty-eight years old before she experienced her first orgasm and now she's enjoying sex more than she ever has in her life. Do you think you aren't orgasmic because you're nervous? Or that you feel you are neurotic and have to solve your emotional problems before you can expect your sex life to be satisfying? No one is totally free of emotional hangups, but despite emotional hangups one can enjoy

sex and be orgasmic too. If you think you have to feel totally
good about yourself, your life, your job and children before
you will be able to experience orgasm, then you may be waiting around forever. This is one reason why traditional psychotherapy has never been very successful at curing anorgas-
mia.[13] Working directly on the mental problems can help to
resolve them, and possibly help in sexual areas as well, but it
is often more efficient to work directly on the sexual problem
if you decide you want to change it. Joan saw a gynecologist
because she could not have orgasms. The physician recommended that she undergo psychoanalysis. For two years she
worked through her problems with her mother, father, sisters,
and brothers, but still never had an orgasm. She started having orgasms only after she came to the women's groups and
learned about her sexual anatomy and about masturbation.

Is it because you're too embarrassed to ask for what you
want at a particular time; afraid he'll refuse, get angry, or
feel emasculated? Is love-making too short and too fast for
you?

Would it be a relief if your doctor told you that you
couldn't be orgasmic? Would it be easier to accept that you're
a physical anomaly? The truth is, you're probably not. According to Helen Kaplan, general loss of sexual interest can
reflect "underlying debilitating illness, fatigue, depression, or
the use and abuse of certain drugs. Fluctuating hormonal
states as during the menstrual cycle or in pregnancy or the
use of contraceptive medication may influence female sexual
functioning adversely."[14] However, cases of physical disabili-
ties that affect orgasmic response are exceedingly rare in an
otherwise sexually responsive female. In almost all cases, if
you have a clitoris, you can be orgasmic if you want to.

But what can you do about it? You may be willing to try
anything, but you may not know where to begin. Relearning
about your sexuality can be enjoyable but requires time and
practice. It means that you have to assume responsibility and
be somewhat assertive. Our culture has taught us that a
woman should depend on a man to take care of her, which
means she can blame him for mistakes. It's nice to be driven
around in a car, but it's also nice to be able to drive yourself
so you can go where you want to, when you want to. But to
do that, you'd have to assume some responsibility. Many
women have been trained into passivity. They've been taught
to hold back, or hide their strengths and desires. Lethargy,

boredom, and feelings of powerlessness can result from not asserting oneself. The cure is not rest and tranquilizers, or the psychoanalyst's couch, but participation. While it's risky to set out to accomplish something by yourself, for yourself, succeeding can be worth it.

According to Ovid's legend, Zeus and Hera were arguing about which one, man or woman, derived more pleasure from sex. Since Tiresias had been both a man and a woman, they called upon him to settle the argument. To this question, Tiresias quickly responded that women did.[15] Perhaps Tiresias is right; we have no way of really knowing since we can't switch sexes. However, there is probably no reason why you can't enjoy sex fully and be orgasmic. Look to the wisdom of your body, your feelings and instincts. After you find out what really turns you on, you can change your sexual practices to fit your responses, rather than attempting to react to the things you think should turn you on. You'll never really know how your subjective experiences compare to those of another person, but if you enjoy your own experience, it really doesn't matter.

2: *Sources of Sexual Confusion*

Until recently, most women have accepted male views of female sexuality. Even when these views may have conflicted with a woman's own self-knowledge, she acquiesced or remained silent rather than challenge the authorities who were predominantly male—researchers, writers, doctors, psychologists, religious leaders, and family breadwinners. Furthermore, many women considered themselves inadequate and abnormal if their experience conflicted with the words of the "authorities."

Freud made the first intensive exploration of the psychological aspects of sexuality and, like many pioneers who approach a totally unknown area, he arrived at some biased conclusions. Freud concluded, ". . . that in the phallic phase of girls the clitoris is the leading erotogenic zone. But it is not, of course, going to remain so. With the change to femininity the clitoris should wholly or in part hand over its sensitivity, and at the same time its importance, to the vagina."[1] In direct contrast to Freud's position, the more recent physiological findings of Masters and Johnson show that no switch in area of responsivity ever occurs and that the clitoral area remains the area most sensitive to sexual stimulation throughout most women's lives.[2]

Until recent years, women who sought the help of doctors for their orgasmic problems often found that their "inadequacy" and "abnormality" was confirmed by their doctors. Members of the medical profession based their judgment of normality mainly on what Freud and others had outlined. Some physicians went so far as to attempt to eliminate the problem by eliminating the clitoris. One theory argued that if the clitoris and its surrounding structures were removed, this area would not interfere with the vagina's sensitivity. Clitoridectomies, as various forms of this operation were called, were sometimes performed on young girls in Europe during the late 1800s to inhibit masturbation, and on young women to prevent unfaithfulness.[3] However, nowhere in the literature do we find recommendations that the penis or testicles be removed to curtail the masturbatory activities of boys, or the adulterous activities of men. One thirty-four-year-old woman who came to the University of California clinic to be treated for orgasmic difficulties had had the hood of her clitoris removed when she was four years old because of excessive masturbation—and that mutilation occurred just thirty years ago!

Women who today seek help from physicians for orgasmic difficulties will not be given a clitoridectomy, but neither are they always likely to be given accurate information or pertinent advice in the area of sexual functioning. The general lack of accurate knowledge among physicians about sexual functioning is easy to understand if one remembers that until very recently, sexuality and sexual functioning were topics largely ignored in the curriculum of most medical schools. Thus, you find yourself seeking help from "authorities," who may in actuality know less about sexuality than you know. They, too, are victims of a culture that subscribes to outdated notions.

Evelyn was married at sixteen and after four years of marriage went to her doctor because she had never experienced an orgasm and felt there might be something medically wrong. Her doctor told her that she did not have orgasms because her sex organs had not quite "matured" yet and that after they did, in a few years or so, she would become orgasmic. This advice was totally inaccurate; female infants as early as four months of age are reported to have experienced orgasm.[4] But Evelyn believed the doctor and, as she waited for this maturing process miraculously to take place, she became less interested in and more resentful about sex. At thirty-five, when she began the group, she was furious at having wasted years before doing something more positive about the problem. One doctor told Judy that she shouldn't concern herself about not having orgasms; that it's not necessary for a woman to have orgasms. When Kim complained to her doctor about not liking sex, he told her to participate because of her husband's needs, because sex was her husband's privilege. One woman was even told by a doctor not to masturbate. He said it was important for her to save all her sexual feelings for her husband—as if masturbation would "use up" all her sexual desire.

Sally was a virgin when she married and when she went to her physician for her pre-marital exam, he informed her about what to expect with intercourse. He told her it would feel like a steel rod being shoved into her vagina and that it would be very painful. Her reaction was to develop vaginismus and dyspareunia. (Vaginismus is the name given for excessive tightening of the muscle of the vaginal opening. Dyspareunia is the medical term for pain with intercourse.) Since she expected sex to be a painful experience, she tensed her vaginal muscles to help guard against the anticipated hurt. Ironically, her attempt to protect herself from the pain actually caused it.

Most sins perpetrated by doctors in the area of sexuality, however, result more from omission than commission. Some doctors just haven't received the necessary training in sexuality to be able to help patients with sexual problems. Sexual dysfunctions are treated as commonplace and benign conditions, possibly in the hope that if the patient stops worrying, her problem will resolve itself. Certainly, orgasmic dysfunction is not a life or death problem, but it is an area of considerable concern to many women. Relieving the over-concern and worry is essential to reversing the situation, but is frequently insufficient in itself.

Western religious and moral upbringing has also been influenced mainly by men since it is men who hold the positions of authority in most religions. Many organized religions have traditionally regarded sex as intended primarily for procreation. Women are seen alternately as sexually pure—the madonna—or basically carnal with sexual appetites that need to be suppressed—the whore/temptress.[5] This confusion between sexuality and morality has been another source of conflict for many women.

So, it is not surprising that many women enter adult sexuality feeling uneasy, embarrassed, unsure, sinful. In the words of sex therapist Thea Lowry, "Psychologists have put a pathological label [frigid] on women who are unable to do as adults, what they were brought up to be unable to do." Many of us received clear messages while growing up that presented sex as bad, dirty, a subject best avoided. We may have been taught that a nice girl wasn't even supposed to know that such a thing as sex existed, at least not until after she was married. Then, miraculously, sex was supposed to lose all its nasty connotations and become a joyful experience.

In our very early years, before we even knew sex existed, many of us were taught not to explore our bodies "down there," and reprimanded if our hands wandered in that direction. We may have been given separate washcloths, one for our face and hands, and one for the unmentionable "other place." The message was clear: it must be terribly dirty and disgusting down there. Ironically, Gloria discovered her orgasm precisely as the result of those negative messages. She put that extraordinarily dirty place directly under the faucet in order to wash it more thoroughly and was pleasantly surprised to find that the pressure of the water created a most intense sensation which culminated in orgasm, although she did not recognize it as such at the time.

Somewhere, either directly or indirectly, we got the message that we shouldn't touch our genitals, and so, when we did, we felt ashamed and confused. Boys were praised for handling their penis when they were toilet trained, whereas girls were diverted from direct genital contact. If we allowed our hands to linger on our genitals long enough, we may have experienced the pleasure derived from touching the clitoris. But we never heard anyone else mention these pleasant sensations. As a result, we may have grown up feeling weirdly unique—as though no other girl did such things and felt such things. Feeling that we must be abnormal, immoral, we would make silent pacts with ourselves that we would touch ourselves just this time and never again; but we were forever breaking this promise to ourselves and to the omniscient God observing us from above. Often, when we did give in, we masturbated as surreptitiously and quickly as possible in an attempt to avoid the feelings of shame and guilt.

Mary grew up with the idea that touching herself "down there" was at least sinful, if not physically harmful. She did not realize that what she was doing was masturbation and was only vaguely aware that it had anything to do with sex. One day, just before taking a nap, she masturbated. When she awoke, she was ill and was sure that the illness was caused by touching herself before falling asleep even though she had done it many times before with no adverse effects. She was so frightened that she avoided masturbating for months afterwards.

The natural curiosity of children includes the desire to explore their own bodies—everywhere—and to explore the bodies of others. In darkened basements with flashlights, out behind the garage or in the grass among the trees, we furtively and curiously examined each other to see how we were similar or different. "Playing Doctor" gave us the thrill of dangerous exploration but also the guilt and fear of being caught—with our pants down, so to speak.

We learned quickly that we shouldn't ask questions about sex or about "that" part of our body which was supposed to remain a mystery to us until marriage. (It is interesting to note that this very area of the body which was so dirty, secret and shameful, was also purported to be the most sacred gift you could give, unsullied, to your husband on your wedding night.) If we did ask about sex, the embarrassment evidenced by our elders quickly convinced us not to ask again. We had only two avenues for our ignorance—books or miscellaneous information gathered from friends.

The most frequent source of misinformation came from peers who rarely knew any more than we did. We may have gotten the egg and sperm story straight, but how the egg met the sperm remained a mystery. Looking to the written authority to help us out wasn't much better. Of course, the greatest authority was the dictionary, was it not? The dictionary method went something like this: We looked up a word we had already heard, but weren't exactly sure about. For example, the word intercourse. The second definition in Webster's New World Dictionary states: "Sexual joining of two individuals; coitus; copulation."[6] Well, we already knew that much, but we wanted to know just exactly how this was done. But here are two new words, coitus and copulation. So we look up coitus and the definition is "sexual intercourse."[7] Nothing new on that round! Copulation wasn't much help either. So maybe we persevered and began again with vagina: "A sheath or sheath-like structure; specifically, in female mammals, the canal leading from the vulva to the uterus."[8] The only thing we've learned is that we don't know what the vulva or uterus is. And so the search continued in this circuitous and frustrating manner.

Being female and fearing disapproval, we carefully kept our sexual curiosity a secret. We learned the traits of being "feminine," to depend on others and to seek their love. Hence, most of us readily learned to adapt, and not make

trouble. To be passive was to be loved. But being passive fr
quently meant giving up control over one's body: learning
trade tomboy tree climbing, no matter how much we enjoy
it, for being the mother of dolls. Girls were praised for bei
clean, pretty, and unobtrusive. Boys were expected to be a
tive, to aggressively explore and confront situations head o
while girls were to be protected, comforted, and cared fo
We were considered too delicate to endure the bumps ar
bruises that exploration inevitably produced. So, trading vig
for prudence, we shaped our behavior to conform to the e
pectation that males are aggressive while females are r
strained. As a result, many of us ended up expecting ov
male partners to be the active initiators in sex while we r
mained the passive recipients.

Being passive and striving for love as a measure of se
worth—rather than making an impact upon the world—
created some traumatic and almost intolerable situations fo
many young girls. This passive stance may have made som
girls particularly susceptible to child-adult sexual contact o
incest which, if it generates enough fear, shame, or guilt, ca
result in orgasmic difficulties later in life.

Whether or not we experienced sexual traumas befor
puberty, the onset of menstruation often caused conflicts an
problems. Some women who had been given no informatio
about menstruation recall that they reacted to the first mer
strual flow with terror: were they hurt or sick? Even if it wa
explained ahead of time, the circumstances rarely seeme
conducive to open and unembarrassed communication. Som
of our mothers handed us books on "growing up" while oth
ers merely left books lying around where we were certain t
find them. This way of handling the topic opened and close
the subject, all in one motion. We quickly perceived that th
wasn't a topic for candid discussion. If Mother actually di
discuss "growing up" with us, usually we felt her embarras
ment, which was in turn the result of her own sexual up
bringing. Even if we did have a solid, communicative rela
tionship with our mothers, we still found ourselves plague
with blood and cramps each month. Ironically, just becaus
we were now "women" and could some day experience th
joy of bearing children, we were supposed to have an elate
response to something which has been nicknamed th
"curse." This prospect seemed a slim reward—especially sinc

we would have to wait approximately ten years to collect. Meanwhile, we remained self-conscious about it all.

Angela talked about putting in tampons for the first time. Studying the diagram enclosed in the package merely added to her already considerable confusion about what her body was like inside. She finally found the courage to insert a tampon, in what she hoped was the right place. She was convinced that it ended up being lodged somewhere between her heart and her stomach. Angela's experience was by no means unique. Sadie inserted the tampon, cardboard container and all, and couldn't understand why the product—which advertised itself as being completely unnoticeable when in place— was so painful. Another group member abandoned the use of tampons just a few months after beginning to use them. She explained that they were just too painful to insert. Somewhere she had gotten the idea that the tampon had to be as far inside as possible in order to work properly, so she was putting the cardboard all the way in before releasing the tampon.

Although some of our mothers felt pride when we menstruated, we felt mainly discomfort. Moreover, after explaining menstruation, many of our mothers gave us no further information about sex; they remained embarrassed and we remained curious. Laura actually had intercousre at the age of nineteen without realizing that it was intercourse. A number of women in the groups experience a good deal of anger, especially towards their mothers, for not providing them with the necessary information about sex or for treating sex as a dirty activity, rather than emphasizing its joyous qualities.

Repressive attitudes toward sex, as we know them, are not universal. According to Ford and Beach, "The societies that severely restrict adolescent and pre-adolescent sex-play, those that enjoin girls to be modest, retiring, and submissive appear to produce adult women that are incapable or at least unwilling to be sexually aggressive ... quite often they do not experience clear-cut sexual orgasm. In contrast, the societies which permit or encourage early sex play usually allow females a greater degree of freedom in seeking sexual contacts."[9] They found that these women when mature are generally more vigorous and aggressive during sex, which results in regular and satisfactory orgasms.[10] Some cultures perform various puberty rites celebrating the development of adult sexuality. The erotic dances that frequently accompany these rites teach the art of love-making in pantomime. Our culture celebrates no comparable rites. However, our children can receive positive messages about sex from the obvious pleasure evidenced by their parents in the affectionate, playful, and loving gestures they extend to one another.

Another major concern of females, from childhood through adulthood, is physical beauty. For a little girl, being pretty, rather than plain, is considered a big plus. Peers responded less critically and adults more favorably if you looked pretty. But as we approached adolescence, our feelings about our physical selves became particularly acute as we watched our bodies "develop" with each passing day. We would agonize and wonder how it would all end up. Would we have large or small breasts? What size would our waist or hips be? Would we always be taller than the boys? And we would constantly compare ourselves to our friends in an attempt to figure it out. While we were developing, it was almost as if our bodies were sabotaging us. We'd suddenly find a breast getting in the way where one had not interfered before. We'd constantly develop new pimples, despite the medications that guaranteed relief or your money back. We felt clumsy and awkward, far from the graceful high school girls we secretly emulated. We felt no security in this new body which was becoming so different from the old comfortable one. We never knew what to expect next, as we asked the eternal question, would we be pretty?

Being attractive was of tremendous importance because it signaled love and acceptance, but it also presented a number of problems. While we longed to be attractive to the opposite sex, we had a lot of ambivalence about actually attracting them. Is it really OK to lure boys or are we bad and promiscuous if we're attractive? The message was always mixed—yes and no. Our parents would respond with pride when we got all dressed up to visit relatives, but with suspicion if we were going out with our friends. The lipstick and eye make-up advertisements promised us popularity, but our wanting to use those products precipitated incessant battles at home. Finally after months or years of fighting, we may have won the right to cover our naturalness in an attempt to be pretty.

Many of us found ourselves overweight and constantly breaking the diets we had designed. Being overweight had its compensations; those of us who were fat did not have to compete in the sexual arenas where stakes were high. We could blame our weight for our lack of boyfriends and could nourish fantasies of how alluring we would be if only we lost the proper number of pounds. But we never put our fantasies to the test by slimming down; possibly we felt safer within the extra inches of armor. At least, we rationalized, we knew that the friends who liked us really liked us for ourselves, for our personalities, and not because of such superficial attributes as looks. These were the thoughts that plagued pretty girls—am I liked for myself, or just for my external appearance?

Thus, appearance and appeal seemed to present a myriad of problems. If we were attractive, we may have worried about alienating other girls who were jealous of our looks, remembering well the lessons learned earlier that success at competition was not a favorable attribute for a girl. If we attracted boys we had the outside affirmation that we were, indeed, desirable, but we also became embarrassed over the attention and felt unsure about handling our admirers. If boys pursued us, we faced the dilemma of "putting out" or being labeled a tease or a prude. If he had an erection, we often felt we had to do something about it because we caused it. Walking the thin line between popularity and promiscuity wasn't easy.

We were led to believe that our sexual feelings for our boyfriends were wrong and bad. Boys were rightfully supposed to like sexual activities, while girls were not. How disconcerting it was to find out that many of us did when we weren't supposed to. So, many of us dutifully learned to keep our sexual feelings well under control or to suppress them altogether. When we were allowed to "date" it was clear that the responsibility for keeping things in line was ours. Boys were expected to "get away" with anything they could while we were supposed to stop them. Their sexuality was sanctioned; but a "good" girl was above sexuality, a cool creature of sensibility who knew not only how to control her own sexual feelings, but her partner's as well so she would not be "taken advantage of." We were taught that only "loose" girls participated in sex and that, while a boy could use these girls for his pleasure, he would never respect or marry a girl like that. A girl who acted on her sexual feelings would get a bad reputation while the boy would get a better one.

When I was a sixteen-year-old high school student I attended a fraternity weekend with a boyfriend who was twenty-one and in college. We were at a New Jersey beach and a beautiful day was coming to a close. As the evening grew longer and we grew more passionate, he earnestly implored me, "Never let me do anything to you that would make me lose respect for you." What a bind! Am I being too free in his eyes? Is this a warning about something he plans to try next? I was frightened and confused. Why couldn't he stop himself? Why did I have to figure out everything and keep the lid on things?

Somehow, after years of practice at turning off sexual feelings both outwardly and inwardly, each of us is supposed to miraculously emerge as a turned-on passionate woman when a legitimized adult sexual relationship materializes. Sally, one of the group members, realized that she desired sex more and felt more sexual sensations at sixteen than she did ten years later when she entered the group. She had learned to turn off her feelings very effectively while necking in the back seats of cars.

For many of us, the floodgates of our sexual feelings did not miraculously open when we finally started having intercourse. Even if our initiation into sex occurred on our wedding night, totally sanctioned by society and our parents, it may not have been easy to erase all the earlier negative messages that kept us anxious, uptight, and over-controlled.

Those of us who decided to go "all the way" before we were married may have had sex to prove our love to a boyfriend, or because we had run out of excuses and, exhausted by male pressure, found it easier to give in than continue to fight. Deciding to have sex because *he* wanted it was a fuzzy decison at best. Did we really want sex too? Would he still respect us afterward? Or would he abandon us in the gutter as we were taught we deserved? And our worst fear was that he wouldn't keep it a secret, even though he had promised he would We dreaded that he might even exaggerate his descriptions in locker room conversations, and that before we knew it, all our friends would know and our reputations would be forever ruined. All of these thoughts could produce enough anxiety and insecurity to prohibit relaxation and enjoyment of our first sexual experiences. Even if we were strong enough to overcome the pressure of society and to decide on our own that making love was what we wanted for ourselves, the decision was often more easily accepted intellectually than emotionally. The 1972 Playboy Foundation Study indicates that more than half of the single females under twenty-five found their first coital experience as neutral or unpleasant. Only 20 per cent said the first time was very pleasurable.[11]

Our first sexual experiences may have been good, bad, or indifferent. However, more than likely, we were self-conscious and embarrassed. Am I moving my body right? Am I making enough noise or am I too loud? Am I sexy? Would he rather be with so and so? And most of all, is he enjoying it and am I making it good for him? Not knowing what was in it for ourselves, we concentrated our energy on pleasing him and figuring out what he wanted us to do. Besides, we'd been much better trained at deciphering what someone else wanted and how to supply it than we were at making requests and obtaining pleasure for ourselves. So we ended up unsatisfied and wondered why there was so much fuss about sex anyway if there was no more in it for us than that. At the other extreme, we may have experienced arousal to such an unaccustomed and intense degree the first time that it may have frightened us. As the rush of novel feelings threatened to overwhelm us we may have frantically fought to maintain control.

Not experiencing satisfying sex today is even more difficult than in the past because of the current demands on women to become sexually liberated. Societal pressure is making it harder and harder to say no, even if we don't feel we're ready for sex just yet. More and more unmarried women are sexually active according to Hunt. Approximately two thirds of the women in his sample had had premarital coitus by the age of twenty-five.[12] But just because more women are sexually active these days doesn't mean that more are deriving adequate pleasure from sex.

Despite more liberal attitudes toward premarital sex, many women find themselves sexually experienced but not experiencing sex as the comfortable carefree experience it has been billed to be. Janice used to laugh as required at a party when dirty jokes were being told; but the laughs were hollow and she secretly wished she knew what she was missing. To her, sex was just becoming a bigger and bigger drag.

An infinite number of events and experiences have contributed to your current sexual experiences; each woman has been affected differently. Knowing how you got to your present situation may help you to realize that you're not the only one who feels as you do. "The Myth of the Vaginal Orgasm" by Ann Koedt, "The Politics of Orgasm" by Susan Lydon, and "Organs and Orgasm" by Alix Shulman are essays which may add additional perspective to the issues presented in these first two chapters.

3: Where Are You Now?

When we have to, we are all capable of finding ways of coping with a sexual situation that is consistently frustrating. Many women have worked out compromises that enable them to endure sexual frustration, but these tend to be purely expedient measures which allow one to maintain a sex life at a bearable level, without actually solving the problem. Do you find yourself in any of these situations right now?

One common tendency is to get into the vicious cycle of expecting a sexual encounter to end with your feeling dissatisfied and frustrated, while hoping that *this* time it will be different. If so, you may find yourself being a spectator of your own love-making. As the love-making continues, you may grow more and more fearful that the orgasm is not going to happen. So you are constantly weighing your responses as you try to attain the elusive orgasm. The more closely you watch and worry, the less aware you can be of what your body is feeling. As your partner begins thrusting, you begin giving up. As he experiences orgasm, possibly you are left feeling defeated, angry, sad, alone.

Ellen would find herself laughing uncontrollably after a particularly frustrating episode of love-making. Betty, on the other hand, would end up crying. But both women, after they had gone through these emotional stages, eventually felt almost nothing when love-making ended. They had learned to live without sexual enjoyment. It is unfortunate, though understandable, that after consistent dissatisfaction with sex, if you can't see a solution to the problem, you begin to treat sex as a chore and attempt to avoid it or get it over with as quickly as possible.

You may find yourself sitting around patiently or impatiently waiting for "Mr. Right." You may be blaming your mother or father for not giving you the information you required or for instilling in you negative feelings about sex.

42

You may be blaming your partner for not knowing enough or not caring enough. Or maybe you are beyond the point of caring whose fault it is, and like many women in the groups, have learned to "turn off" sexual feelings in an attempt to protect yourself from the inevitable frustration resulting from another incomplete sexual experience. The earlier you turn off, the less frustration you may feel in the end. Some women learn to turn off so promptly that they experience no pleasurable sexual feelings at all.

Needless to say, under these conditions, the quicker sex is over, the better. You may have become an expert at making him come as quickly as possible. You know all the techniques that will excite your partner to orgasm, and you concentrate on these in order to get the love-making over. The faster he comes, the less time you are compelled to endure intercourse. But the more you focus on hurrying his orgasm, the less you concentrate on your own experience. If you turn your sexual feelings off at the outset, there is no possibility you'll ever have an orgasm because you do not allow yourself to build on the small feelings you might experience if the process were to develop more slowly.

The most common method women use to cope with not reaching orgasm is to fake it. Many men will say that they don't believe a woman could successfully fake an orgasm, that they are certain they can tell the difference between a real orgasm and a faked orgasm. But can they really? Women have been faking orgasm successfully for years. But how can a woman learn how to fake an orgasm if she has never experienced a genuine one? Toni Ayres, one of my co-workers, learned by reading pornographic novels. The heroine would breathe hard, make deep gurgling sounds in her throat, and writhe about. So that was what she used to do. Carmen faked so successfully for two years that her partner never knew she wasn't orgasmic. She must have faked very convincingly, because even after she became orgasmic, she swore he couldn't tell the difference. He only noticed that she seemed to be enjoying sex more than ever.

Why do women fake orgasm? The reasons vary. Carmen and other women faked orgasm so that a partner wouldn't think they were inadequate. Do you fake because you're embarrassed and ashamed because you never have orgasms, or don't with any frequency, and you may not want anyone, especially your lover, to know. Maybe you're afraid he'll reject

you. You may want his approval and think that responding to
him sexually is one way to gain it. Another reason many
women fake orgasm is to protect a partner's ego. Ellen's partner would try so hard to bring her to orgasm, she said that
she just didn't have the heart to let him down. You may
somehow feel it's your duty to validate a partner's masculinity by showing him that he can satisfy you sexually. If you
don't, you may fear he'll feel inadequate, be depressed, possibly even leave you. Still other women fake orgasm just to
get the man to stop. If you know that a considerate male
partner is trying to last until you achieve orgasm, and you
know you aren't getting any closer, you may fake it—another
technique to make him come so that you can get him to stop
thrusting and leave you alone.

But what price do you pay for faking orgasms? First, you
may be so busy faking that you end up totally missing the
sexual feelings that you might otherwise perceive. After one
group series was over, Janice said, "You know, I was faking
so much, that it's possible that I had an orgasm, a little one,
and didn't even know it." A second difficulty is that faking
prevents your partner from learning that a problem exists.
Unless you let him know that something is amiss, he will assume that his love-making techniques satisfy you. Consequently, he will continue doing the very things that have not
been working. If you could let him know what is happening
he might be willing to join you in trying out techniques that
would prove more satisfying.

Finally, faking can be a trap because once you begin, it's
hard to stop. The fear is that if you tell your partner he'll explode into rage or dissolve in hurt. Possibly you worry that
he may feel he can't trust you again. But while there is a risk
in admitting you've been faking, it's probably not so great as
you might expect. If you explain yourself in a straightforward
way, but without blaming him, chances are good that he'll respond with kindness and concern. However, if you tell him in
anger, in the midst of a fight, you can expect the worst.

Sarah finally gained the courage to tell the man she had
been living with for a year that she had never had an orgasm
during that whole time. This couple had a particularly active
sexual life. They frequently made love twice each day, and
each time he would have two or three orgasms. He felt that
he had to perform this way in order to satisfy her. When she
told him that the thrusting of his penis was not the most sexu-

ally exciting thing for her, he was incredibly relieved. He then admitted that he had been faking some of those second and third orgasms because he thought that his coming inside her was what really turned her on. Thus, a double fake was in process. Both were trying to live up to what they assumed the other's expectations were, and consequently did not enjoy sex as much as they did after that talk. When they slowed things down and tried more manual and oral stimulation, they started having one orgasm apiece and enjoying sex more.

Many women compromise by participating in sex for a partner's sake. Making love enables one to feel close to a partner. Most of us enjoy seeing a partner feel good and look happy. But that pleasure is often canceled if you feel yourself stiffening up as the cuddling turns into love-making.

You really can get more out of love-making than feeling close to a partner, seeing that a partner is happy, however important these things are. There is no reason why you cannot find as much satisfaction in sex, on a regular basis, as he does. You should be able to get as well as give. Lydia enjoyed feeling close to her lover, but she said she always felt somehow cheated. You, too, are likely to feel some resentment if you are making love mainly for your partner, rather than for yourself, constantly seeing your partner enthralled while you usually remain only lukewarm.

It is only to be expected that women whose love-making entails faking, giving only for another, wind up viewing sex as a chore, a duty which is performed only in order to have children or to keep a husband or lover from straying.

Women avoid sexually frustrating situations in various ways. Since it is frequently difficult to say no directly, your body may do the job for you. You may get headaches, or backaches, or be too busy during the day and too exhausted at night to make love. You may develop a vaginal infection; perhaps you forget to take your pills, or run out of foam, or neglect to insert a diaphragm. All of these can be ways to avoid love-making. You make yourself sexually unappealing with mudpacks, curlers, baggy pajamas, or possibly you provoke a quarrel just before bedtime. Unlike a man, unless a woman refuses verbally or uses physical ailments as an out, her body is able to participate sexually even if she's not sexually aroused. For men, the penis can say no. Nevertheless many men, and even a greater number of women, endure the emotional and physical discomforts of making love at times when they're not really interested.

Of course, it is possible to find some pay-off in using unsatisfactory sex as a way of punishing your partner. You don't have an orgasm and he feels sorry, or by grudgingly going along with sex in a passive and disinterested way you keep him from enjoying sex as much as he might if you, too, were really involved.

Where does all this leave you? Even though the media, the women's movement, and new contraceptive availability has changed some attitudes, it still may leave you feeling inadequate and insecure about trying anything new. Perhaps you don't want to broadcast your own "deficiency." Or, you may be left sacrificing your own pleasure in order to please a partner, protecting his ego so he won't feel inadequate. It almost surely leaves you demoralized, without a solution to the problem. Maybe you're convinced you will never enjoy sex fully or reach orgasm.

If you are caught in any of these binds, there are solutions, and we'll explore them in the chapters to follow. Since sex is just a basic form of communication and lack of sexual communication may be indicative of other communication failures in your relationship, it may be best to begin by discussing the problem with your partner, just as soon as you feel ready to, so that your partner understands what's going on and can join you in seeking a solution. But most of all you need to decide to *do something about it yourself*, beyond complaining and waiting for your partner to take action, or waiting for some miracle to occur. Trying new things is the first big step. For example, is intercourse really the only way to make love? What are some of the things you might suggest to a partner that might help? Some of the exercises in Chapter 8, 9, 12, and 13 are one approach, but it's up to you to do the talking, to take the initiative. By understanding where you are now, and seeing how your particular ways of coping with sexual frustration actually prevent you from solving the problem, you may find the courage to experiment and change your sexual life. Masters and Johnson have helped redefine sexuality by describing the actual process of the sexual response cycle in women. Each woman needs to build on that basic information (contained in Chapter 5) and discover her unique sexual pattern; and then share this knowledge with her partner.

4: The First Steps Toward Change

I talked with a colleague, Leah Potts, about the many negative sex messages and experiences women have to overcome in order to become more sexually responsive. "You know," she said, "the whole thing just wouldn't seem worth the effort—except that it feels sooo good."

One way to get beyond the negative sex attitudes you may have developed is by finding out what they are and, if possible, where they come from. Certainly, you may not be able to unravel all the tangled strands; some of the messages may have been so indirect they remain only vague feelings which you are unable to trace back to anything specific.

But nevertheless, there are a number of ways to go about re-exploring your sexual past. One good way is to sit down with a close female friend and describe to one another sexual attitudes and experiences you had while you were growing up. The women in the groups found this exercise especially helpful. By talking with another woman, as opposed to a man, it is easier to reach a deeper level of understanding because of the common history of growing up female. Although a man might be able to appreciate and understand you, his understanding would not be based on his personal experience. Nonetheless, there are some advantages to discussing your sexual history with a good male friend, or lover, too. Doing so can make the relationship closer and more intimate; it can deepen the level of trust between the two of you; it can give you further understanding of what has gone into shaping the personality of the person with whom you are so intimate. Opening up communication through an intimate discussion of your sexual history can provide a good starting point for the two of you to begin discussing sex more openly with each other and for understanding one another's needs and difference. If there is no one with whom you feel comfortable discussing these issues, try writing down your thoughts. Or, at

47

least set aside some time alone in which to explore your thoughts in depth.

The following topics should provide a good starting point for exploring your attitudes and development as a sexual being: 1) What were your parents' attitudes toward sex? Your mother's? Your father's? How were they communicated to you? 2) What was the attitude of your peers toward sex as you were growing up? 3) When and how did you learn about menstruation? What was the attitude of the person who told you? Were you frequently very uncomfortable—cramps? Were you ever embarrassed by an incident involving menstruation? 4) When and how did you learn about masturbation? Do you remember when you first masturbated? 5) When and how did you learn what sex really was? Were you shocked? 6) What were the circumstances of your first real sexual experience and what was it like for you? 7) Any sexual traumas such as child-adult sexual contact, rape, or other frightening sexual experiences? Spend five to ten minutes on each question. (For additional exercises of this nature, refer to Roberta and Herbert Otto's book, *Total Sex.*)

Some colleagues found that another area of exploration which proved to be very important to the women in the groups was a direct discussion with their mothers about sex. Telephone your mother or visit her if either is possible. Begin the discussion by asking her what *her* mother (your grandmother) told her about sex and contraception when she got married. This information can be productive for a number of reasons. First, it can help to put your mother's personal attitudes toward sex in perspective—especially if they have been negative. Second, you may learn some things about your mother and her sexual attitudes which may differ from your expectations, and this may enable you to re-evaluate your impressions. Third, this discussion can grow in breadth and depth including early experiences, conversations, events— things you may have forgotten about or things you always wanted to share but never had the opportunity or courage to initiate. Most importantly, it can give you a real framework, negative or positive, in which to view your sexual development. This aspect of placing fantasies in perspective can be a very positive learning experience.

In the *Sensuous Woman*, "J" wrote: "Pin up on your bed, your mirror, your wall, a sign, lady, until you know it in every part of your being: We were designed to delight, excite, and satisfy the male of the species."[1] I would like to add that we were designed to be delighted, excited, and satisfied ourselves. Nina always had a smile on her face and never voiced any dissatisfaction to her husband. She always tried to make the best of things and totally withheld anger and disappointment. She feared that if she expressed any negative feelings he would stop loving her. She was so practiced at withholding all her feelings that her sexual feelings never got expressed either and she never experienced an orgasm. It was amazing to her that when she began to express some of her pent up feelings in other areas of her life she began orgasmic expression of her sexuality as well.

You deserve pleasure, but pleasure may be a hard thing to allow yourself to take. It's possible to feel you don't deserve it or that other things are more pressing or important, so you leave yourself out.

Developing your sexual potential means finding time to devote to sex; for most women this means allotting the time from busy schedules. But to make the time and accept pleasure, you have to feel you deserve it, that you are important too, as important as those you love and care for. It's necessary to give to yourself as well as to others. If you always have to be the good, strong, giving one, you can't help being angry at times about always getting the short end of the deal. Sarah had been well trained to wait on men and she was good at it. She was a good seamstress, a good cook, and a caring and selfless companion. But she ended up resenting her partner and the fact that he thought he could repay her by making love to her. Without even realizing it, she found herself thinking, "You think you're so hot, I'll show you. I won't have an orgasm." Surely there are benefits from being a selfless, martyred servant. Because you wait on him he is indebted to you. Perhaps you'll be worth so much to him that he'll never risk leaving you. But you could be getting more for yourself as well. It's unlikely that he stays with you just because you're a good servant. Ellen was angry at her husband but kept being the good "wifey," as she put it. In the group Lydia told Ellen: "You've got a right to live. You're not serving time. Be good to yourself. Be kind to yourself. You deserve it. It's a matter of survival." Lydia added that she had always thought it was better to give than to receive. "I used to give things away to be liked. You know, that's a bunch of horseshit. I deserve something for myself too."

You have a right to refuse things you don't want and ask for things you do want. You may feel you deserve and want more for yourself, but how can you begin going about having your needs met? Here is an exercise that has been beneficial to virtually every woman with whom I've worked.

The exercise is called Yes's and No's. Doing the No's entails saying no to three things you didn't want to do anyway. It could mean saying no to someone who has asked you to do something that you don't really want to do. For example, one of Ann's No's was to a woman from a charity who wanted Ann to go out collecting money for them. Ann always hated doing it, but had never refused before. This time she did and felt relieved. It can also mean saying no to yourself. In other words, you can refuse to do something you feel you *should* do but don't want to do. For example, Laura always cleaned her house on Saturdays, but on this particular Saturday, she was exhausted from a busy week and just didn't feel like doing it. She really felt like going out shopping instead and so she said no to the "I should clean house" and enjoyed her day.

Try saying no to at least three things in the next few days. You can say no to yourself or to someone else, but it's important to do at least one of each. Sarah always felt she had to go to bed with the men she was steadily dating, even if she didn't want to on a particular night. She was afraid if she refused that she would lose them. She decided to take a risk and began telling her lovers, before she even went out for the evening, that she did not want to have sex for a while and that she would tell them when she felt like it. To her amazement her request was honored and respected. One lover did try to push her to make love, but she held firm and not one man ended the relationship because of her refusal to have sex for the period of time she needed to feel that she was back in control of things.

The Yes's are just the opposite of the No's. Doing the Yes's entails saying yes to three things that you really want but would not normally let yourself have or would not usually allow yourself to ask others for. Eve splurged and bought herself a sweater she had been admiring, but felt was too expensive to buy for herself. Barbara asked her husband to make dinner one night when she was tired. She had never considered asking him to do something like that before. Joy was going to be thirty-five in a week and felt this was a very important point in her life. She asked some of her friends if they would make something special for her for this birthday and ended up receiving some beautiful hand-crafted gifts.

Experiment with the Yes's and No's and see how you feel after doing them. Remember, you should select things you would not normally allow yourself to refuse or request. If you would have said yes or no anyway, it doesn't count; the point of the exercise is to try to help you do some things differently, to be more self-assertive. Some women can perform the No's easily but have difficulty with the Yes's. For other women the problem is just the reverse, and many women have trouble with both. Practice the one(s) you have difficulty with a few times more. Don't berate yourself or become discouraged when you realize that you let an opportunity go by. Missing opportunities is a good way to see just how often you fail to permit yourself the freedom to do or not to do things. You may see how much of yourself you deny for others. Louise thought that doing the Yes's and No's would be easy for her. She felt further ahead of the other women in the group. Then she realized she had a stomach ache. She said, "If I let myself, I'm going to get in touch with all the things that are similar to the other women and it's going to be hard and may take a while." Each woman must begin where she is and go at her pace. Only you know how far and how fast you can push yourself without considerable discomfort.

Feeling you deserve more for yourself is necessary for developing your sexuality. If you don't feel you deserve the pleasure, you won't set aside the time necessary to attain it. If you don't set aside the time to practice, nothing will change.

In addition to opening up your feelings about your sexual past, and feeling you deserve more for yourself, it is imperative that you get back in touch with your body. Any alienation you may experience can be as much the result of socialization which taught you to keep your body discreetly covered, as the media messages which dictate how you should look. (We are bombarded with ads that ask: Are you clean and hairless? Do you smell just right in all the proper places, or should you buy such and such a product to enhance your appeal?) Have you ever stopped to think just who you are grooming for? Is it for you, for him, or for the advertising agencies?

You may be alienated from the sight of your body. When

was the last time you really looked closely at your body? Many of us avoid looking because we see only the imperfections—imperfections which magazines, television, movies, etc. have taught us to recognize. Mass media, and designers of women's clothing, set different standards for what a woman should look like each year. If she's not this year's model, a woman is made to feel dissatisfied, and she may put herself down. Women accept that blatant fallacy that unless they look like a twenty-year-old Playboy Bunny, they're not sexually attractive. Wide hips were "in" one decade and large breasts the next. Now in the seventies we're all expected to be flat-chested beanpoles. If your body type is "in" one year, it's "out" the next. To try and rearrange your body to fit the times is, of course, absurd. Few people applaud the natural body changes that accompany the processes of aging and child bearing. It's time to stop thinking that the problem lies within ourselves and start wondering why the media is trying to cut all of us out with the same cookie cutter rather than encouraging us to capitalize on our uniqueness.

Very few of us have the current "ideal figure" and there is no reason why we should even attempt to conform. It's important to get to know your own body, to become friends with it even if there are a few improvements you would like to make. The women in the groups found the process of really experiencing their bodies in a new and different way an invaluable one.

How can you get back in touch with your body? One good exercise is to set up a full length mirror in the privacy of your room. Lock your door and undress in front of it. Carefully examine your body. You might talk to yourself while you're looking, telling yourself what you see. Look at your body from all angles, standing, kneeling, sitting with legs apart and together. Look at yourself for a minimum of fifteen minutes. Seeing what your lover sees when he looks at you might make you less embarrassed and inhibited. Some women are preoccupied with making sure the lights are out and that their bodies are safely hidden under the covers before they can relax and get into a sexual mood. When a partner does caress your body do you remain concerned about whether he likes it or not? Do you have a tendency to rearrange yourself to keep what you consider your worst attributes concealed? Playing the artful dodger is certainly not conducive to a relaxed, open, and enjoyable sexual encounter.

If you feel your partner has negative feelings about your body or is not quite comfortable with it, you might try asking him about it and discussing it together. You may learn that you're far more critical of yourself than others are of you or you may learn that you have very realistically appraised the situation. You may want to change things and you may not. In any case, talking about it directly together can help keep things in perspective.

Many women in the groups at first had difficulty carrying out the mirror exercise. Expecting the worst, they procrastinated to avoid confronting their fears. However, few women in the groups found the actual exercise to be as disconcerting as they had expected. Most women have not looked at their bodies for so long that their negative expectations are far out of proportion to the image reflected in the mirror. Cindy did not want to do the mirror exercise because she was a bit overweight. We pointed out that just because she avoided looking didn't mean the weight would not be there. It was important for her to know the body she walked around in each day, even if it was changing. Eventually she carefully studied her body, and to her surprise, she found that she actually liked it, despite the extra weight. Cindy rarely goes on diets now. The few extra pounds don't seem to make so much difference now that her attitude about her body has changed and she has learned to accept it. Some women find that looking at their own body really turns them on. Once one gets over feeling guilty, or that it is somehow egotistical and narcissistic to enjoy the body's appearance, you may feel free to enjoy your body much more.

After you've examined yourself carefully in the mirror for at least fifteen minutes, begin to explore your body with your hands. Again, try talking to yourself about what your hands are feeling. Ms. Jeremy Brav made this suggestion to the women in one of her groups: "Pretend you're from another planet landing on this unknown body for the first time. Your assignment is to explore this new body completely." Run your fingers over your arms, legs, stomach, etc.; feel the muscles, the bones, the fat, and the varied textures of skin. Compare the skin on your inner thigh to that on the soles of your feet, to that on your lips, ears, chest, shins, buttocks. Enjoy the feelings of your hands touching your skin as well as your skin being touched. See if you can't discover something you didn't know before. Do you like any areas better than you thought you would? Can you begin to accept the fact that it's OK to look the way you do? Leslie told the group, "I feel a whole lot better about my body. We're not quite good friends yet, but we're friends."

Understanding and accepting the way you are now—your mind and how it has developed through upbringing and experience, your body and how you look and feel physically— are the first steps toward understanding and accepting yourself as a person with a unique sexual nature.

5: The Anatomy and Physiology Involved in Female Sexuality

In order to understand how a woman functions sexually, it is important to distinguish between the various parts of the female genitals, and to see how each part works. The following is a very brief description of female sexual anatomy to help you locate the various structures; the diagram in the Appendix can be used as a guide.

The most external structure of the female genitals, the fleshy outer lips (labia majora) are covered with pubic hair. Within these outer lips are the inner lips which cover the vaginal and urethral openings when the woman is not sexually excited. At the point at which the inner lips are joined together at the top, there is a small pink structure, varying in size, but often about the size of a tiny pea. This structure is called the glans of the clitoris, and it is a very important structure in female sexuality. It may be difficult to find the clitoris at first because it is covered by a hood called the prepuce. Like the shaft of the penis, the clitoral shaft extends from the glans of the clitoris beneath the hood. Below the clitoris and above the vaginal opening is the urethra. This small hole, through which urine is expelled, is also sometimes difficult to locate. The easiest way to find it is to put your finger inside your vagina and pull the opening down toward the anus. The urethra will generally appear from within the folds of skin. Below the urethra is the vaginal opening. The area between the vagina and the anus is called the perineum.

The illustration on page 56 shows one woman's genitals. Each woman's genitals are unique. That is, while women have the same basic structures, these structures vary considerably, from woman to woman, in size, color, shape; and the structures vary in distance from one another. The genitals have a configuration as unique as our faces have: we all have eyes, a nose, and a mouth, but they vary in size and placement. Some of us have large noses, but this doesn't mean we

Clitoral
Hood

Head of
Clitoris

Inner Lip

Outer Lip

Urethral
Opening

Vaginal
Opening

can smell better; small eyes don't mean inferior vision. These differences, however, do play a part in making each of us unique in appearance. The same is true of the genitals. The "faces" of a person's genitals are different. However, the size or the placement of the different structures does not seem to have much effect on sexual functioning.[1] Some women have large puffy outer lips while others have very thin outer lips. In some women the outer lips take on a hue that is just slightly darker than the area around it. Some women have a lot of pubic hair and others have little, and the color of a woman's pubic hair can differ in color from the hair on her head (just as the color of the hair in a man's beard often differs from the color of hair on his head).

The size of the clitoris also varies somewhat among women. In some African tribes little girls elongate the clitoris either through pulling or some other artificial method because a large clitoris is supposed to be a sign of beauty. Some women have a small bump on the glans of their clitoris; or their clitoris is split, resulting in two separate but attached pieces. The hood over the clitoris can vary considerably in size and fleshiness. The clitoral hood of some women has many folds while others are very simple and small. The inner lips vary as well. Some women have very narrow inner lips, while others have long inner lips that hang below the outer lips. The inner lips vary in color from pink to brown; and some women even have two-toned inner lips—pink on the inner part with brown toward the edges. None of these variations seems to affect the ability of a woman to respond sexually.

One of my favorite stories is one I heard from an artist friend. As a young girl she examined her genitals and found that one of her inner lips was longer than the other. She assumed that this must have been caused by masturbation. Rather than stop masturbating, she decided to concentrate the stimulation on the side that had the smaller inner lip and, in this way, attempt to even them out. As you might have guessed, she never did succeed in evening out the lips. The discrepancy wasn't caused by masturbation, but was one of the unique features of her genitals.

Now that the various areas of your genitals have been designated, it is important to understand the ways in which these different structures function sexually.

For most women the urethra is one of the least important

structures from the point of view of sexual stimulation. Stimulation of the area just outside the urethra can be enjoyable and sexually arousing for some women, while others just find it irritating. The urethra usually goes unnoticed in most women until some bladder infection or infection of the urethra develops which can cause misery. It may itch or burn, irritate in a way that makes the woman feel that she needs to urinate, even if she doesn't have to. Infections of this type and other gynecological disorders can often be prevented by two simple health techniques. First, after you go to the bathroom, wipe the anal and vaginal areas separately to prevent bacteria in one area from infecting the other. The second health technique pertains to a common infection women contract when they first begin to have sexual relations; called cystitis, it is sometimes known as "honeymoon cystitis." If you are prone to urinary infections, the best way to control cystitis and similar problems is by drinking water before intercourse and urinating before and after having intercourse. This cleans out the urethra and helps to prevent infections from occurring.

The vagina is just below the urethra. The closeness of these two structures may account for some of the confusing messages girls received while growing up. Since most of us didn't know there were two openings down there, we associated the entire genital area with urination. Urinating was something private and we were always apologetic when we excused ourselves to go to the bathroom. So it is possible that at some level we ended up confusing our sexual and excretory functions.

The erotic sexual sensitivity of the vagina varies with the individual woman. However, nerve endings that respond to touch are only contained near the entrance.[2] Therefore, the walls of the first third of the vagina are more responsive to sexual stimulation than those of the inner two thirds. The inner two thirds is sensitive to stretch and pressure,[3] and many women get considerable pleasure from this area during the deep thrusting which takes place during intercourse. Since it is the outer third of the vagina that is most sensitive, however, almost any penis is large enough to stimulate this area. Even though the size of an erect penis, regardless of its size when flaccid, varies very little from man to man,[4] it is true that some women have a preference for a larger or a smaller penis. But this preference varies with the individual woman, it's not generally based on the anatomy of the vagina. A large penis does not make a man a better lover.

This idea of preference in sexual matters is a very important one. We accept the idea that different people prefer certain foods; preferences for certain foods reflect individual differences of constitution, temperament, or past experience. The same holds true for preferences in sexual stimulation. Individual preferences may have nothing to do with how your sexual organs respond. There are differences in the actual quantity and specific types of nerve endings existing in the various areas of each woman's genitals;[5] these anatomical differences may account, in part, for the difference in sexual preferences. Preferences can also be learned; they can result from the experiences of touching yourself, information, and misinformation resulting from things you've read or from what friends have said. You may be capable of having orgasms in a number of positions, but prefer, for whatever reasons, a particular position. Your task is to discern or begin to learn about your unique preferences in sexual stimulation, as you do every day in food or dress.

Another important physical characteristic of the vagina is the large muscle that surrounds the opening; it also covers the whole pelvic floor (from the pubic bone to the tail bone). This is called the pubococcygeal muscle, or "PC muscle," and it is one of the muscles that contracts during orgasm. If you put your finger into the entrance to your vagina and/or the entrance to your anus or both during an orgasm, you usually can feel this muscle contract. This muscle may be lacking in tone in some women, especially after childbirth. Like any other muscle, the PC muscle needs exercise to keep it in its best condition. A series of exercises popularly referred to as "Kegels" were developed by Dr. Arnold Kegel for women with the common problem of urinary incontinence.[6] These women would expel urine when they sneezed or coughed and these exercises were designed to tighten the PC muscle, and hlp them contain the urine. Many gynecologists recommend these exercises routinely to women after they have had a baby.[7] "Kegeling" is also taught in many natural childbirth classes.

Some of the women who followed Dr. Kegel's advice reported that after about six weeks of practicing the exercises they experienced increased pleasure during sexual intercourse. The women I have worked with have also found that exercising this muscle increases sensitivity in the vaginal area. In addition, strengthening the PC muscle helps reduce spontaneous urination with orgasm, an occurrence which is not unusual among women. I highly recommend that you practice the following Kegel exercises.

To locate your pubococcygeal muscle, urinate with your legs apart; the muscle you squeeze to stop the flow of urine is the PC muscle. Practice stopping the flow of urine a few times in order to become familiar with the muscle. Then, lie down and put your finger in the opening of your vagina and contract the PC muscle. See if you can feel the contraction around your finger.

After practicing the following exercises for about six weeks, see if you notice any difference in the strength of your PC muscle when you put your finger in your vagina and squeeze.

The first Kegel exercise consists of squeezing the PC muscle for three seconds, then relaxing the muscle for three seconds, and squeezing it again. At first, do ten three-second squeezes at three different times during the day. It may be difficult at first to keep contracting for a full three seconds. If that is the case, contract for one or two seconds and build up the time as the muscle gets stronger. The advantage to these exercises is that you can do them anywhere and at any time and no one can tell you're doing them. Practice when you stop the car for a red light or in the morning when you wake up. Or do them when you answer the telephone at home or at work, or when you are lying down to rest. The muscles surrounding your anus may also move during the exercise, but if you find that you are moving your thigh muscles, your stomach or buttocks, you are probably squeezing the wrong muscle.

The second exercise is like the first except that the objective is to squeeze the muscle, release it, squeeze again and release as quickly as possible. This is nicknamed the "flutter" exercise. Again, squeeze and release ten times at three different times during the day. When you first start doing this exercise, it may feel like a tongue twister; you may not be able to tell if you are contracting or releasing and for a while it may keep getting muddled all together. However, after working at it slowly, you will gradually be able to do the flutter more rapidly.

The third exercise consists of imagining that there is a tampon at the opening to the vagina and that you are sucking it up into your vagina. Gloria was actually able to suck water into her vagina and then spurt it out again when she did this exercise while taking a bath.

The fourth exercise consists of bearing down as during a bowel movement, but with the emphasis more on the vagina than the anal area. This exercise is more apparent to an observer. Both the sucking in and the bearing down should be held for three seconds, as with the first exercise.

All four exercises should be practiced ten times each at three different times during the day. As you progress with these Kegel exercises, slowly increase the number in each series until you are able to do twenty of each exercise in succession. You can do them as frequently during the day as you can find time, but consider three times daily a minimum.

If you notice some discomfort or tightness in the pelvic area at the beginning, reduce the number of daily contractions, but do not abandon the exercises. Like any muscle that is being exercised for the first time, it may get a little stiff at first. It is quite important to keep this muscle, like others in your body, in tone. The exercises can become as much of a habit as brushing your teeth and, like brushing your teeth, they should be continued for the rest of your life.

The anus is also a very sensitive area for some, but not all women. Some women enjoy having this area lightly stroked or licked during love-making. Some women enjoy the insertion of a finger in the anus while having intercourse and others enjoy having their partner's penis inserted into the anus instead of the vagina.

But for many, if not most, women, the most important site of sexual sensitivity is the clitoral area. Recent research indicates that two thirds of the "normal" women studied preferred and responded more readily to clitoral than vaginal stimulation.[8] The fact that the clitoris is usually more sensitive to sexual stimulation than the vagina is because the density of nerve endings in the clitoris is far greater than it is in the vagina. Kelly was relieved to learn this fact since it explained her lack of sexual feelings. She said that it was good to know that it wasn't her fault that she had been feeling very little sexual excitement during intercourse.

The entire area above, to the sides, and below the clitoris is generally highly sensitive to sexual stimulation. However, the exact areas that provide the most pleasure differ from

woman to woman. Embriologically, the glans of the penis
and glans of the clitoris developed from the same tissue.[9]
Therefore the glans of the clitoris itself actually has a higher
density of nerve endings than does the glans (or head) of the
male penis.

The clitoris has no other function than that of providing
the woman with sexual pleasure.[10] Laurie, a very religious
woman, had some initial difficulty accepting the fact that it
was the clitoris and not the vagina that was the primary seat
of sexual excitement in most women. She explored the area
with her fingers and found it to be true for her. Since the clitoris has no function other than providing sexual pleasure,
she reasoned that God must have meant it to be there so that
the woman would enjoy sex. Otherwise God wouldn't have
put it there. Laurie's explanation seems to persuade other religious women with whom I have subsequently worked that
sexual pleasure and religious morality are compatible.

The inner lips are attached to the prepuce or hood covering the clitoris and to the clitoris itself. During intercourse,
the thrusting of the penis in and out of the vagina pulls on
the inner lips which in turn pull on the hood and the clitoris.
This movement of the hood back and forth over the sensitive
clitoris provides sexual pleasure for most women during intercourse. Check this for yourself by tugging on the inner lips
and by inserting several fingers in and out of the vagina.
Since both the vaginal and clitoral areas are being stimulated
simultaneously during intercourse, it is often difficult for
women to discern exactly where the pleasurable stimulation is
coming from. Once the importance of the clitoris is understood, it is easy to see why the indirect stimulation of this
area provided by intercourse is frequently insufficient to enable a woman to reach orgasm. The clitoral area may also receive stimulation from the rubbing of the male's pelvic bone
against the clitoris, but again, this nonspecific stimulation may
be insufficient to enable a woman to have an orgasm through
thrusting alone. Many, if not most, women require additional
direct stimulation of either the glans or the shaft of the clitoris
or the adjacent areas. It makes no more sense to justify the
necessity of direct stimulation of the female sex organ, the
clitoris, than it does to justify the need for direct stimulation
of the male sex organ, the penis, in order for an orgasm to
occur. Somehow, we have accepted the myth that additional
clitoral stimulation, beyond that provided in intercourse,

should be unnecessary or is unnatural. The belief is that the penis should produce the orgasm; but if the penis does not produce enough direct pressure to stimulate the woman's most sensitive area it seems sensible to add stimulation that does.

Some women find it difficult to slide the hood back and forth easily over the clitoris. This can be caused by the gathering of natural secretions called smegma which can get trapped under the clitoral hood where they may dry and harden if the area is not washed regularly. These crystals of smegma can make clitoral stimulation painful. The effect is similar to rubbing your eyelid when sand is caught underneath. Smegma can be removed by washing the area. In a small minority of women, tiny membranes called clitoral adhesions can attach the clitoris to the hood preventing the hood from moving freely back and forth across the clitoris. By using a dull probe, a doctor can sever these attaching membranes in a simple procedure in his office. It has not been satisfactorily established, however, whether this minor operation plays an important part in enabling a woman to experience orgasm.[11] Some women do report having been helped by this procedure; however it is difficult to determine the extent to which improvement resulted from the power of suggestion. Many women with clitoral adhesions experience no difficulty having orgasms. Again, different women respond differently.

Psychological or physical stimulation is required in order to reach orgasm. There are a few women, about 2 per cent of the population according to Kinsey, who are capable of having an orgasm through fantasy alone, with no accompanying genital stimulation; another small percentage can experience orgasm through breast or other non-genital stimulation.[12] Some women have experienced spontaneous orgasms and many women have had orgasms while dreaming. However, despite these exceptions, a substantial amount of stimulation of the genital area is the necessary prelude to orgasm for most women. The exact area and type of genital stimulation needed for orgasm depends upon the physiological make-up and learned response patterns of each individual woman. Let's assume that two women have comparable emotional involvement with a man. His love-making technique might arouse the first woman, but exactly the same approach and type of stimulation might do nothing for the second woman.

Again, we are talking about preference. Some women prefer direct and hard stimulation of the glans of the clitoris or the surrounding area, while others find this kind of stimulation irritating and enjoy a lighter touch. Preferences for timing and sequence, for setting and mood also vary from woman to woman. As my co-worker Leah Potts puts it, "If you want to make beautiful music with me, you'll have to learn my song."

Physiologically, an orgasm is an orgasm, whether it occurs during masturbation, intercourse, oral stimulation, or any other form of stimulation. The subjective experience may differ, but the physiological cycle a woman goes through as she builds sexual tension, reaches orgasm, and returns to the initial resting place is the same for all women. This process, called the sexual response cycle, was detailed by Masters and Johnson as the result of the scientific observation of numerous women in their laboratory in St. Louis, Missouri.[13]

For purposes of description Masters and Johnson divided the sexual response cycle into four general phases: the excitement phase, the plateau phase, the orgasmic phase, and the resolution phase. These phases are not totally discrete. There is no distinct end to one phase before the next phase begins. Instead, the phases represent an effort to describe a sequence of reactions that characteristically occur in what is really a continuous process.

Before sexual excitement commences, the female sexual organs are in what is called the resting state. The inner lips are flaccid, covering the vaginal opening; the vagina is more a potential space than an actual space. Like a balloon that has not yet been inflated, the walls of the vagina are relaxed and touching.

As the woman becomes sexually aroused through fantasy, emotions, contact with her lover, self-stimulation, or any other form of stimulation, the excitement phase begins. Bloods starts to accumulate in the pelvic area just as blood accumulates to make our faces red when we blush.

In addition to the engorgement of the sexual organs with blood, a number of other processes occur during the excitement phase. One of the first noticeable signs of sexual excitement is the presence of vaginal lubrication. Through the use of a clear phallic-shaped camera which was inserted into the vagina during masturbation, Masters and Johnson learned that most of the lubricant was actually exuded by the walls of the vagina in a process similar to sweating. This lubrication process, a response to the rise in vaginal temperature produced by increased blood supply, is one of the first signs of sexual arousal in a woman, just as an erection is one of the first obvious signs of a male's arousal. Lubrication is generally present internally before it reaches the vaginal orifice. Anxiety, contraceptive pills, certain drugs, hormonal changes are some of the influences that can inhibit lubrication even when a woman feels turned on. In these cases saliva or K-Y Jelly can substitute for vaginal lubricant. The presence of lubrication does not necessarily indicate that the woman is sufficiently aroused to want intercourse to begin, although many men interpret the presence of lubrication as a signal for penile insertion. And it is certainly no indication that a woman is close to having an orgasm. She might be able to have intercourse at this point without it being unpleasant, but it would probably be much more pleasurable if she waited and continued other forms of stimulation first.

As sexual stimulation continues, the vagina expands and lengthens. The elastic capacity of the walls of the vagina are impressive. The vaginal space can compress enough for the walls to hold a tampon snugly and expand enough to permit the birth of a baby. As the vaginal canal expands, the uterus, which naturally extends into the back of the vagina, tips forward and up providing enough space to accommodate a penis. The most common cause of the discomfort that can sometimes occur during deep thrusting is the impact of the penis against the mouth of the cervix. The cervical mouth itself is not very sensitive, but contact with it can cause the attached uterus to move, and the resulting pressure on the ligaments which hold the uterus in place may cause the pain a woman sometimes feels. Switching to a coital position that avoids this contact can help eliminate discomfort.

The accumulation of blood in the pelvic area causes the tissues to swell in much the same way a sponge swells when it is filled with water. The outer lips, inner lips, clitoris, and sometimes the breasts, begin to look puffier and slightly enlarged in size. In some, but not all, women the nipples become erect. Late in the excitement phase, the darker skin surrounding the nipples, called the areolas, begin to swell also.

As the sexual excitement continues, the female experiences some changes that are characteristic of what Masters and Johnson call the plateau phase. The outer lips may become even puffier as she approaches orgasm. The tissues of the walls of the outer third of the vagina, including the PC muscle, swell with blood and a narrowing of the space at the vaginal opening results. The affected area is called the orgasmic platform. This constriction of the vaginal opening can intensify the pleasure of the male partner because his penis, when inserted, often feels as if it is being snugly held. At about this time, the clitoris may appear to be lost somewhere beneath the hood; you may wonder where it has gone and search for it in order to continue clitoral stimulation. However, the clitoris does continue to respond to direct stimulation of the area around it.

The breathing and pulse rates increase. A so-called "sex flush" may become visible at some point during the plateau phase, but it doesn't appear on everyone. This flush is a measle-like rash which generally appears on the stomach, breasts, shoulders, neck, or face area. The extent and description of the sex flush varies widely among women. The areolas surrounding the nipples may swell even further. Sometimes this area swells to such an extent that, in comparison, the nipples do not even look erect. Many muscles—the facial muscles, thigh muscles, hand and foot muscles may automatically and noticeably tense up. Many women consciously tense up even further the muscles in the pelvic area, the buttocks and thighs, to heighten their sexual pleasure.

The above descriptions generally accompany the plateau phase, but the extent to which each sign is visible depends upon the individual woman and to some extent the particular situation. The one definite and dependable sign of an imminent orgasm is a change in the color of the inner lips, not the easiest sign to discern during love-making. For women who have never had children, the inner lips turn from pink to bright red and, in women who have had children, from bright red to a deep purple or wine color.

After this change in color, if effective stimulation is continued, the woman will move into the orgasmic phase. Breathing, pulse rate, and blood pressure will continue to rise until a body reflex reverses the process of progressively increased muscle tension and blood supply to the sex tissue. You cannot force an orgasm any more than you can force a knee jerk; both reflexes just happen naturally. The mounting muscular tension and engorgement of blood vessels reaches a peak and orgasm occurs. The first third of the vaginal barrel, the PC muscle that has formed the orgasmic platform, contracts rhythmically every 0.8 second for a brief period. The number and strength of the contractions vary in accordance with the intensity of the orgasm. The muscles of the uterus, and possibly the anal sphincter muscle, will also contract more or less strongly. These contractions may be apparent externally as the abdominal area appears to contract in waves or spasms. In many women, these contractions are barely, if at all, noticeable. The orgasm may be accompanied by a reflex grasping-type muscular response of the hands and feet. Some women may experience a feeling of warmth emanating from the genital area. This sensation of warmth results from the release of the blood from the engorged blood vessels of the pelvic region. The orgasm triggers the release of blood, allowing it to return to other areas of the body, and the resolution phase begins.

Regardless of what type of stimulation the woman receives, her body will progress through the physiological phases of the sexual response cycle. Whether the orgasm occurs through clitoral stimulation alone, through manual masturbation, through use of a vibrator, through love-making with another female, as the result of intercourse with a male partner, or fantasy alone, the reactions that comprise the cycle of excitement, plateau, orgasm, and resolution will proceed as described. The Freudian distinction between the "vaginal" and "clitoral" orgasm does not match scientific findings. Every orgasm manifests itself in the whole pelvic region regardless of the part of the body that has been stimulated. If you have an orgasm once through intercourse alone with no accompanying direct clitoral stimulation and another time through oral sex, it would be erroneous to label the first a vaginal orgasm and the second a clitoral orgasm. Both are simply orgasms. Both involve the same set of responses. The subjective experience of the orgasm may vary according to the woman's mood, her feelings about her partner or about masturbation, the duration of stimulation, etc., but the physiological process of the build up and release of sexual tension remains more or less the same. In the words of Masters and Johnson, "From an anatomic point of view, there is absolutely no difference in the responses of the pelvic viscera to effective sexual stimulation regardless of whether the stimulation occurs as a result of clitoral body or mons area manipulation, natural or artificial coition, or, for that matter, specific stimulation of any other erogenous area of the female body."[14]

Since orgasm is usually triggered by genital, and more specifically clitoral, stimulation, the excitement usually stops if the stimulation stops. Stopping the stimulation does not cause the excitement level to diminish completely, but it will ebb until effective stimulation is reinstated. Effective stimulation can be anything that arouses you. If it doesn't arouse you, it is obviously not effective for you. Consequently, you may be very turned on by manual or oral stimulation before intercourse and feel very close to having an orgasm, but once intercourse starts, and the focus shifts to vaginal stimulation by the penis, you may experience a drop in the level of arousal. Although you may enjoy the physical and psychological experience of intercourse, you may not be able to reach orgasm. Again, this experience does not hold for all women, but a drop in excitement can occur because the kind of stimulation that was arousing you before intercourse was replaced by another kind when intercourse began. Women who have had a number of experiences of this nature may often find themselves turning off when intercourse begins because they have learned to equate intercourse with the end of the more intense stimulation.

Effective stimulation is generally required up to and during the orgasm; if stimulation is discontinued during the orgasm itself, the orgasm may stop abruptly before completion. This incomplete release can be an intensely frustrating and unsatisfying experience. So let me repeat: consistent, continuous stimulation of a type dictated by individual preference is required to bring a woman to orgasm.

Women's experience of orgasm tends to vary. Orgasm has been described as a "rush," "a mint-flavored heat wave," like "one heartbeat all over," or a "misty cloud that envelops me." Marion describes her orgasm as "this pleasurable thing that flows over me and I feel like I'm flowing down a river—feeling warmth, and for a short time I lose all thoughts of everything." Gloria has a different experience. She says, "I sort of feel this feeling—I feel this build-up, then there is this feeling after it that's different, that's distinct—and I don't feel contractions, but I don't feel like going on any more. And I feel relaxed."

The resolution phase describes the return of the sexual organs back to their accustomed resting state. The swelling of the areolas subside and as a result the nipples may appear even more erect. If a sex flush has occurred, it now disappears. Sometimes a fine film of perspiration appears over the body. There is general relaxation of muscular tension. The uterus and clitoris return to their normal resting position. Some women experience a soreness of the clitoral area for a few moments after orgasm. The vagina returns from its ballooned state back to being a potential space.

This return to the normal, unstimulated state may be completed within a few moments to half an hour after the occurrence of orgasm. If orgasm does not occur, the resolution phase can take an hour or longer. When orgasm does not occur, the length of time required for the completion of the resolution phase will usually be determined by the level of arousal attained during the plateau phase. The greater the arousal, the longer the time required for resolution. Women sometimes complain that increased congestion of blood in the pelvic region may leave them feeling bloated and uncomfortable when orgasm has not occurred. This feeling of discomfort may last for several hours after sexual stimulation has been discontinued.

Some women are capable of being stimulated to orgasm again before the resolution phase has been completed. Women with this capacity have been labeled multiply orgasmic. According to Sherfey, many, if not all women, are potentially capable of having multiple orgasms during one sexual encounter.[15] Most men require periods of time ranging from a few seconds or minutes, usually in young men, to thirty minutes or several hours or even days in older men before they are capable of a new erection and subsequent ejaculation.[16] Some women do not seem to experience any such refractory period, whereas other women do seem to have a normal refractory period of some duration before they are capable of a second or third orgasm; other women feel complete after one orgasm. The response may also vary depending upon circumstances.

When Kinsey first published *Sexual Behavior in the Human Female* in 1953, a great furor took place over his disclosure that 14 per cent of the women he interviewed claimed they were regularly capable of responding orgasmically two, three, and even more times during one sexual encounter.[17] Critics claimed that this was an impossibility and that Kinsey had been taken in, and these women were really frigid.[18] Masters and Johnson have subsequently found that some women are capable of more than one orgasm within a fairly short period of time if continually stimulated.[19] However, an innate capability may bear no relation to what is satisfying for the individual woman. You may be content with one orgasm or have two on rare occasions. Perhaps if you have any more than that, you may find the process more unpleasant than rewarding. On the other hand, you may be capable of experiencing and enjoying a number of orgasms in sequence. Regrettably, the recent emphasis on multiple orgasms has made many women feel inferior or inadequate if they prefer to experience only one orgasm. And this expectation adds a tremendous burden to the woman who rarely, if ever, experiences orgasm and now is expected to have three or four.

What is important is the woman's own pattern and her satisfaction with it. Some women reach orgasm quickly, while others respond more slowly. Many women have one strong orgasm, others have a number of mild ones, and many levels exist between the two extremes. In some women the first orgasm is strongest and the rest are milder; or the first is the mild one, the second more intense, and if there are more, they may vary in intensity. What fits for you may not fit for someone else. One way of responding is not innately superior to any other. However, people often think that "the grass is always greener" elsewhere. We expect that what we don't experience is really better than what we do experience. One can certainly remain dissatisfied and disappointed if one wants to, especially since there is no way to experience what someone else experiences internally. However, the investigation of options (see Chapter 9) with no expectations can be a way to explore the range of your orgasm, but enjoying your own sexual response and being comfortable with that response is the most important thing.

Many of us have difficulty identifying whether or not we have had an orgasm. We've been told, "You'll know it if you've had it." If we don't know it for sure, we figure we haven't. We look for signposts. Do we have a sex flush? Can we feel any vaginal contractions? Does our clitoris swell? Do our nipples look erect afterward? Dr. David Reuben says that nipple erection is a sure sign of orgasm: "Erection of the nipples always follows orgasm in the female. In spite of heaving hips, lunging pelvis, passionate groans—no nipple erection, no orgasm. It is an accurate mammary lie detector for those who insist on the truth."[20] However, Dr. Reuben cites no source for his pronouncement. Masters and Johnson, who did the major research in this area, make no such claims. In fact, nipple erection after orgasm is not universal and its absence is no sign of deficient response.

Physiological signs are not the measure of a subjective experience. Perhaps you don't know if you're having orgasms because you're looking for the wrong signposts. Do you end up feeling relaxed—not exhausted, but relaxed? When you masturbate, when do you choose to stop? Because you're frustrated? Because you've set aside a specific amount of time and it's over? Or because you feel satisfied and feel no need to continue? Feelings of satisfaction, relaxation, warm glow are the signs to look for, whether or not vaginal contractions, nipple erection, and sex flush are present or noticeable.

The following are some descriptions by different women in the groups of their subjective experience of the sexual arousal and release process. Harriet writes:

Not having had an orgasm until I was an adult influenced what I thought orgasm was. Finally achieving orgasm was a tremendous positive experience, but the sensation of orgasm itself was fleeting, not as earth-shaking or powerful as I had anticipated. More frequently experiencing orgasm has shown me they vary considerably in intensity, duration, type of contractions, and thoughts leading up to orgasm. For me orgasm is a wonderful pleasure. My body feels very powerful and I feel powerful enough to face problems that seem insuperable. Let me describe my orgasm on two levels ... my mind and my body. My mind anticipates the future relaxation as my imagination savors the release of tension. Then, as I begin to stimulate myself my body takes over. I concentrate very hard on not losing the good feelings of sexual tension focusing mostly in my pelvis, but all over my body. As the stimulation continues I feel rich, warmer and warmer, more and more myself. Suddenly I feel only in the clitoral area and feel as if I want to suck with my whole body. Thoughts are there but they are second to feelings like a magnificent animal. Then contractions begin and sometimes end quickly or continue. As they end the orgasm is over suddenly. I feel so good yet often wish it had lasted longer. Usually my tension is gone and

I can sleep refreshed, but sometimes thoughts take over again. My orgasms make me feel more myself than any other single experience. They are real power and pleasure.

Carol expresses her experience this way:

In an orgasm I tense my muscles, my feet and hands, grimace, my middle (torso) convulses. Then I feel lightness in my head and a relaxing warm feeling. The feeling is one of well-being, spent.

Kelly uses a beautiful image to describe her experience:

As soon as I begin rubbing [my clitoris] I get a pleasant ticklish feeling, and whenever I hit an especially sensitive spot, my whole body jerks slightly. After five to ten minutes of rubbing, a new sensation takes over and I know I am about to have an orgasm.

The best analogy I can use to describe this new sensation is that I am standing on a deserted beach watching a tremendous wave on the horizon coming toward me. This wave gradually comes closer and closer and becomes bigger and bigger until it reaches me and washes over me. As the wave actually hits me, I reach orgasm and a graph of that sensation would be similar in shape to an open umbrella. At the most intense seconds of orgasm, I feel as if I am going up along the shaft of the umbrella and when I reach the point of the umbrella, I feel as if I am coming back down on all sides of the open umbrella. Afterward, I feel very tired and relaxed, and in ten minutes or so I feel ready to start again.

With this accurate information about your genitals and the way in which the sexual response cycle proceeds, the next step in learning about your responses is to become familiar with your own genitals. Spend half an hour carefully examining your genitals with a hand mirror. If you feel uncomfortable doing this, spend only a few seconds looking at your genitals in a dim light. Later on, look for a while longer. Build up the time and the intensity of the light until you have examined all the structures carefully. Label the parts of that special face (using the illustration in the Appendix as a guide) by touching all the areas with your fingers; see if you can determine any differences in sensitivity. Notice the colors and textures of the areas. Place your fingers inside your vagina both to feel the pubococcygeal muscle that surrounds the opening and to see if some areas are more sensitive to touch than others. Some women find pressure placed at the front part of the vagina most pleasurable. Other women are more responsive on the right, the left, or the area closest to the anus. Do you notice any differences? No part is likely to be very sensitive until you are more sexually aroused, so don't be concerned if you don't feel much at first. Later, as you begin to explore more intensely, the differences will become more apparent and you may find that sensations vary from time to time. In any case, the more familiar you are with your own genitals, the easier it will be for you to share them with your lover in a comfortable and self-accepting way. It is important to examine your own genitals carefully and locate all the structures. It is interesting that although we have examined most of the other areas of our body, few of us have ever looked closely at our genitals. By not examining this area, we perpetuate the mystery of sexuality and prevent ourselves from really understanding how our genitals work. When I suggested to one group that they examine their genitals at home, Sherry was stunned. She had been planning a visit to the doctor to find out if she had clitoral adhesions. The idea of exploring her own genitals had never occurred to her.

Some women expect to find their genitals ugly and disgusting. Somewhere in our history we picked up this message. Given society's stress on cleanliness, we have been made to feel ashamed and embarrassed because our genitals are damp and have a slight but distinct natural odor. There is no reason for women to feel ashamed of their genitals. The advertising industry has offered us deodorant sprays to keep the genitals dry and sweet smelling. These sprays can cause more harm than good. Women have found that some of these sprays can irritate the very sensitive membranes of this area and cause considerable discomfort.[21] Similarly, washing your genitals too thoroughly with soap, especially deodorant soap, can also cause irritations or vaginal infections. The best solution is to wash the genital area thoroughly and regularly with warm water especially if you're prone to gynecological problems. If there is no infection present, the genital area will have no more than a slight, natural odor.

You have examined your body and your genitals carefully and completely. But there is more to orgasm than just physiology. What is happening up in our heads is at least as important as what is taking place in the pelvic region.

6: Psychological Aspects of Reaching Orgasm

Sexual arousal consists of more than just physical genital stimulation. Genital stimulation is usually necessary for producing a satisfying and orgasmic sexual experience, but all the stimulation in the world may not produce an orgasm if desire is absent or your attention is elsewhere. If your mind is focused on sexual sensation, your body can enjoy it more fully. Outside distractions, anxiety, anger, operate to divert attention from sexual pleasure and can end up diluting the sexual experience.

If you're angry at your partner and don't want to have an orgasm; if you're afraid or uncomfortable in the sexual situation; if you're tired from a long, hard day; if you've been immersed in your work and can't get it off your mind; if the children cry in the next room or if the telephone rings; or if you're preoccupied with other thoughts, your mind may prevent your body from experiencing orgasm. This will not necessarily prevent you from enjoying the sexual encounter, but these and many other circumstances can block your ability to respond orgasmically.

In one of the group sessions, Harriet recalled that she was able to respond to the point of orgasm more quickly if, before she began love-making, she checked to make sure the children were asleep, the front entrance light was out, and the telephone was off the hook. Having removed these possible causes of distraction, she could relax and enjoy the sexual stimulation more completely.

Kinsey[1], Kaplan[2], and Fisher[3] all refer to distractions, fatigue, and preoccupation as being the most pervasive barriers to a woman's enjoyment of a satisfactory sexual experience. It is important to be aware of the role of distraction because unwittingly one partner may introduce into the sexual situation stimuli which neither person may recognize as being a source of distraction. Interruptions in love-making for a cigarette or sip of wine can lower a woman's level of general arousal. Or, you may turn on some music to help you relax and unwind and to enhance love-making only to find the music may provide sufficient distraction to prevent the attainment of orgasm.

Sally found that the music she chose to play while masturbating interfered with sexual arousal. She would get so involved humming the songs and singing the words that she would forget about the sexual feelings. Women differ in the way they respond to sounds. Some women find that some sounds help build sexual excitement. Connie found that when she heard her children calling, she knew that she had to have an orgasm now or never and just knowing that helped her reach a climax.

There are techniques which you can use to overcome the diverting effect of outside distractions if you are susceptible to them. "White noise," a constant drone of undifferentiated and monotonous sound such as running water, a fan, a hair drier, or vibrator may help to relax both partners and drown out external distractions as might the record *Environments,* which has the sound of the ocean roaring on one side and birds singing on the other.

Other props and techniques such as relaxation, the use of fantasy, erotica, and techniques of focusing attention on the physical sensations work as mental aphrodisiacs to block external distractions while acting as a sort of lubricant which helps to get sensual and sexual messages flowing.

Erotic stimuli, or "mental or psychological aphrodisiacs," are psychological inputs which help to put you in a sexual mood and keep you there. A romantic candlelight dinner or quiet talking in front of a roaring fire can be arousing preludes to sex. Pictorial representations of naked men or women; pornographic films and written pornography that explicitly describe sexual activities are helpful to some women. During sex you might find that concentrating on memories of past erotic incidents or fantasies of sexual encounters you might or might not ever perform or the visual input of your lover's nude or semi-nude body may aid in keeping you focused on the actual sexual situation that is in progress. Attending to these psychological aphrodisiacs can help divert your mind from competing thoughts and orient your mind and body, your total self, toward sexual pleasure.

In the 1940s, Kinsey found considerable differences between a man's ability and a woman's ability to use fantasy, visual erotic stimuli, and written pornography as sexual enhancements. Men were far more responsive to these mental aphrodisiacs while women tended to respond more readily to romantic, rather than explicitly sexual stimuli.[4] A dozen roses, dinner by candlelight, light body stroking accompanied by passionate kissing may be as sexually stimulating, or more stimulating, than thinking about intercourse or actually engaging in it. Exclusive dependence on romantic stimuli for sexual arousal may produce some problems, however. First of all, it may not always be possible to plan ahead and prepare a romantic scene. Sexual desire may arise on the spur of the moment, possibly just from the comfort and warmth of your lover's body lying next to yours. Secondly, roses may put you in the proper frame of mind for sex, but more explicit sexual stimuli may be necessary for orgasm.

According to more recent research, the above-mentioned differences in response to erotic stimuli appear to be more a result of early conditioning than an innate difference in psychological make up of men and women. The Playboy Study found that "women today are far more likely to be aroused by erotic materials and fantasies ... than was true only a generation ago."[5] A study done by Schmidt and Sigusch with "relatively sexually emancipated" and sexually experienced college students at the University of Hamburg showed no significant difference between the response of young men and young women to erotic material, both visual and written, although over all the men reported feeling slightly more aroused than the women.[6]

The results indicate that it is possible, if not probable, that women can, perhaps with broadened experience, recondition themselves to respond positively to erotic stimuli. In fact, many women in the groups found this to be true. Women who had never been exposed to either graphic or written pornography, and had never used fantasy as an adjunct to sexual stimulation either while alone or with a partner, began to experiment. Several women found explicit pornographic movies and novels highly stimulating. Others have been able to fantasize sexual scenes which were very erotic to them. Fantasy did not always come easily initially, but some of the women became more and more able to develop their imaginative abilities in this direction, with very rewarding results.

Feeling sexual and erotic in your mind as well as your

body is important to orgasmic release. Retraining yourself to be more erotically responsive means experimenting for a while until you can tell which particular modes of erotic stimulation will enhance your individual sexuality. The three most common mental aphrodisiacs used by women are: fantasy, pornography (both written and graphic), and total concentration on the pleasurable sensations occurring throughout the body and especially in the genital area.

A major advantage of fantasy as an aid to physical sexual stimulation is that it requires no equipment and is always available. Most of us have been endowed with minds that are creative enough to manufacture fantasies out of thin air. We all do some daydreaming. We may have fantasized about getting to know a handsome man we passed walking down a street; about getting a new job or promotion that may be imminent or only remotely possible; or about the vacation that doesn't begin for another two months. Before getting married, how many of us have fantasized about our future lives with our husbands? These and many other fantasies occupy some of our free time as we relax and let our mind wander; they are acceptable fantasies. Still, many women feel guilty if their fantasies become sexually explicit. We have been so well trained to think that anything sexual is unacceptable that we feel guilty—either promiscuous or over-sexed—if these thoughts enter our minds, and many of us may fiercely guard against their occurrence.

Since women rarely share their sexual fantasies with one another, they have little with which to compare and contrast their sexual fabrications. *My Secret Garden* by Nancy Friday is not a scientifically documented account of female fantasies, but rather it is an interesting compilation of fantasies reported to the author by various women. This book gives an idea of what fantasies of other, very normal women, are like. Reading this book may help you to accept your own fantasies and to be less judgmental about them. It may also give you some themes to incorporate into your own fantasy life if you care to.

A fantasy is simply a creation of the mind. A marvelous quality of the human mind is that it has many levels of awareness. In our subconscious we can explore with dreams. In our conscious minds we can function in everyday life. The imaginative area is in between—under our control, but not totally real—where we can create our own thoughts for the

pleasure that they produce. Combining the pleasure of the
mind and the pleasure of the physical senses in sexual activity
can result in a more intensely enjoyable experience. Fantasy
can be fun, and, like dreaming, provides a release for the
tensions produced by our lives. We can spend our time and
energy analyzing our fantasies if we want to, or we can just
enjoy them.

Having a fantasy does not mean you will want to act it out
in reality. As a matter of fact, in the women's groups we
have found that by giving women "permission" to enjoy and
indulge their fantasizing abilities, they actually become less
afraid that they will act out these impulses unless they con
sciously choose to do so.

Even though fantasy is a natural and normal activity,
many women who fantasize while masturbating or during sex
with a partner may feel guilty for a number of reasons. This
guilt usually has more to do with content of the fantasies
than with the actual act of fantasizing itself. We can experi
ence guilt either because of the sexual acts we imagine per
forming, or the people we choose as fantasy partners.

A very common concern centers around the identity of the
people with whom, in our fantasies, we are sexually involved.
If the imagined lover is a woman, we fear we are terribly ab
normal or possibly latent homosexuals. However, lesbian fan
tasies are not uncommon among women, and they make
sense. Women are attractive and erotic beings. An aroused
woman is sexually exciting. Many of us wonder what a sex
ual experience is like for two women together if we've never
had same-sex experience even if we may have no real desire
for a lesbian relationship. It is only natural to allow in
thought the things one might not feel comfortable expressing
in real life. After all, two women, both of whom are comfort
able expressing their sexual feelings to each other, will find
their love-making just as erotic and exciting as a man and a
woman find theirs. Through fantasy one is free to explore the
whole gamut of human sexual expression.

Women commonly experience concern when the lover in
the fantasy is not the real lover or husband of the woman
who is enjoying the fantasy. He may be a friend, a boss, an
acquaintance, a stranger, or even a relative. Carmen felt terri
bly guilty because her fantasies during masturbation and even
during actual love-making with her lover involved other men.
She agonized about her fantasies because she considered ab

solute sexual fidelity a must in a meaningful relationship. She felt she was unfaithful because her thoughts were of other men, even though she had no intention or even any real desire to sleep with the men in her fantasies. She became more comfortable when she realized that her mind was allowing her the variety that was totally unacceptable to her in reality, especially when she saw that she did not really get sexually involved with other men as a result.

Often we don't allow ourselves the freedom to fantasize during love-making because we feel this must mean we do not find our partner sufficient. Darlene had been married for twenty-five years but still felt guilty if the mere sight of her husband undressed was not sufficient to turn her on. She felt that her love for him should in itself make his nudity automatically arousing to her. In actuality human beings do not respond in this fashion. In time we become used to seeing our partner naked and nakedness is no longer linked in our emotions only with sexuality. We might enjoy spicing up our sex life with fantasies of other lovers whether or not we would ever live out the fantasy. Fantasizing about other men or women cannot be interpreted as proof that we are tired of our real-life lover. Ask your male partner if he ever fantasizes about other women when he is making love to you. Most men will tell you that, on occasions, they do fantasize about other women or previous sexual experiences, something that adds to their enjoyment while taking nothing away from yours. If we accept fantasy while making love or at other times as a perfectly healthy and natural experience it can serve us well. Some women confide their fantasies to their partners and sometimes they keep them entirely to themselves. Many couples find swapping fantasies during love-making very stimulating. If you think you might enjoy sharing your fantasy life with your partner, you might ask him how he feels about it first and act accordingly.

The most common detrimental effect of fantasy occurs when women conclude that they must be perverted if their fantasies contain any unusual sexual acts. In reality, many fantasies contain elements of what some would consider perverse. For example, one of the most common themes in the fantasies of women revolve around rape or forceful seduction. Generally, the woman fantasizing is being taken by force and required to submit to the desires of her seducer/rapist. The guilt here is triggered by the fact that the woman is enjoying the rape and is becoming highly aroused while imagining it. This, of course, conflicts with her intellectual awareness that she should not enjoy this form of sexuality. Actually, if she were really being raped she would probably not enjoy it or become aroused by the act, but safely within the confines of her mind she is free to enjoy the titillation and possibly the pain without threat to her person.

A second common theme that may cause women distress is the reverse of the last theme. In these fantasies, it is the woman who is the aggressor and her partner is a mere servant or slave who is only there to administer to her needs and desires. She takes all the pleasure and gives nothing in return. Beth experienced considerable self-loathing because she always appeared to need this fantasy to reach orgasm. She said, "The men in my sexual fantasies have no meaning to me. They are there solely to give me pleasure. As I become sexually excited, I zero in on my own feelings and nothing else is important to me. My lover is merely an object, rather mechanical, who is there just to create the sexual feelings. He feels nothing for me and I nothing for him. I end up feeling worthless because he is so cool and uninvolved with me and I have been so inconsiderate of his needs." Beth had considerable trouble accepting her fantasies. She felt there was something perverted about her total concern with her own sexual feelings to the exclusion of her partner. She felt selfish. Once she was able to allow herself to get into the fantasy wholeheartedly, to accept it and go along with it rather than fighting, succumbing, and feeling guilty, she began to feel better about that fantasy. She no longer wasted her energy on fighting the fantasy. She could allow herself to relax and enjoy the selfish feelings without feeling guilty and soon she found she was able to become aroused through the use of other fantasies as well.

Scenes of orgies, mate swapping, or a *ménage à trois* are frequent fantasies. Scenes including animals and spanking, whipping, or other sado-masochistic acts are not uncommon either.[7] The numbers of different and diverse fantasies that I have heard have led me to expect the unexpected and I have found no particular connection between the type of fantasy and the personality of the woman.

It seems only natural that we should imagine the illicit during sexual fantasy, for hasn't sex and everything associated with sex always been somehow illicit? Why don't we stop psychoanalyzing our fantasies. Try enjoying the fantasy fully and freely and see if anything changes for you. Also, fantasies change over time. What is exciting this month may become mundane as new and different sexual turn-ons are explored. Fantasy is clearly one of the ways you can widen your sexual experiences without actually indulging in acts that may be unacceptable to you. It is also a very positive way to focus your mind during sexual activity so that you can concentrate completely on sexual pleasures. Not all of us have the ability to fantasize with ease at the beginning, and few of us will ever experience an orgasm by fantasy alone, but you may be able to develop the ability to fantasize which may greatly enhance your sexual feelings.

Erotica—literature, pictures, or movies—can also be mental aphrodisiacs, but they are not frequently indulged in by most women. Traditionally, pornography has been created by men to appeal to masculine tastes, and written accounts of sexual activities are frequently inaccurate as far as female sexuality is concerned.

Many erotic films or erotic photographs may fail to appeal to women, partially because the fantasies portrayed in them are likely to be male fantasies that exploit the female. Women are depicted as perfect bodies. No attention is given to women's other attributes. Also, pictures of naked women may or may not be a turn-on for some women.

Another reason women may fail to respond to such films is that they were taught not to. At best, pornography was something indulged in by college men at bachelor parties and at worst by drunken lechers in sordid theaters. Many women, when exposed for the first time to hardcore pornography, either written or graphic, were really taken aback or overcome with embarrassment or disgust. Many of the women I have worked with responded to their first experiences with pornography with intense laughter. Mostly because of their embarrassment, very few reacted at first with sexual arousal. If one is trained to believe that displays of sexuality are perverted and distasteful, one responds accordingly. Janice saw a pornographic movie for the first time and was very uptight and uncomfortable during the showing. She claimed, "I hated the film, but couldn't wait to hop into bed afterward." She thought she was probably more turned on by the film than anyone else in the audience, even though she was not aware of these feelings at the time. However, despite the constraints

I have described, many women can allow themselves to feel turned on and enjoy a pornographic film.

Considerable misunderstanding and hurt feelings can result from attitudinal differences between men and women about visual stimuli. Many males don't understand why their female lovers do not respond to the display of the male body and genitals. The lack of positive response from a female partner may lead the male to feel rejected and question her love for him. Meanwhile, the female may consider his display distasteful and may think him perverted or vulgar. Similarly, many women take offense when their male lover seeks additional stimulation through pornographic materials. A woman may wonder why her male partner is not fully satisfied sexually with her alone and may fear he is losing interest in her. The male partner, on the other hand, cannot comprehend why she is not similarly aroused by the pornographic material. Open discussions with your partner about the things you find erotically stimulating can be very enlightening. It is important to recognize existing differences and levels of comfort where each of you is starting so that these differences do not cause hurt feelings and rifts in an otherwise positive and happy relationship. Just because you state where you are now doesn't mean you have to stay there. You can slowly broaden your experience if you wish to.

The difference in male and female response to written pornography is similar to the difference in response to graphic sexual portrayals. In general women seem to respond more positively to love stories than they do to more explicit depictions of the sex act. Again, this may be the result of early conditioning. It used to take Jane one and a half hours of constant genital stimulation with a vibrator before she could have an orgasm. In the group we suggested that the women experiment with some pornographic novels while masturbating. Jane came back in the next session reporting that with the aid of the pornography, she could have an orgasm in ten minutes or less. The same results have been reported by other women who required a tremendous length of time to reach orgasm either manually or through the use of a vibrator. This is not to say that your goal should be to have an orgasm as quickly as possible, but if you require over an hour of constant clitoral and genital stimulation in order to reach orgasm, it's very likely that it's because your head is elsewhere. Reading pornography can help to block out other distracting thoughts and worries while keeping your mind focused on the sexual stimulation.

It is easy to see how pornography can be read while masturbating, but it might be more difficult to see how it can be used with love-making. There are many ways to incorporate pornography into partner sex. Reading to each other can be arousing or reading together silently can put you in the mood for sex. One person can read aloud or silently while the other can engage in body caressing and other physical stimulation.

As with other accompaniments to sex, a frequent fear is that the use of pornography is abnormal or perverted, that one becomes addicted to using this method and will not be able to make love without it. But, there is nothing more perverted or abnormal about using fantasy or pornography to enhance sex than there is in using a special perfume or a sexy négligée. They can all enrich the love-making. The major difference is that the use of perfume and négligées appear to be more acceptable to society. But really, your sex life is private and no one except your partner need approve of the things you like to do while making love.

Some women are prevented from experimenting with pornography by their reluctance to go into a store and buy it. Certainly walking into an "adult" bookstore in a sleazy part of town may present a disagreeable experience. Most women feel embarrassed; you may be the only woman in the store. But if you watch the men, it turns out that they are equally embarrassed, if not more so by your presence, and will turn their backs to the aisle and bury their heads in their magazines as you walk by. You need not confront the "adult" bookstores, however, because many pornographic novels are available in regular bookstores. Victorian novels in particular, such as *Fanny Hill* and *The Pearl,* can be found almost anywhere.

Different types of pornography appeal to different women. Some may like the Victorian pornography, with flowery words and descriptions, while others may prefer the more blatant novels chock-full of four letter words. Jenny claimed that the "nastier" the novel the more she liked it. If you try reading pornography a few times and find that it does nothing for you, then you can reject it. But if you've never really experienced it, how do you know for sure?

Unquestionably women can appreciate mental aphrodisiacs. It may just entail acquiring a taste for different erotic material than you may have been exposed to before. There are few non-Greeks who immediately love the taste of retsina, a resinated Greek wine, but after a few attempts at drinking it, it becomes familiar and much more pleasant. Soon the taste may become so enjoyable and distinct that unresinated wine, though good, may seem dull in comparison. Then again, some people never develop a taste for retsina and prefer another type of wine. The same is true of fantasy, pornography, and other erotic adjuncts to sex. It may take time to develop a taste for some of them or all of them, but there is a good chance they can enhance your sexuality if you do take the time to experiment with them.

Another way to occupy your mind with sexual thoughts so you don't get distracted by nonsexual things while making love is by focusing on the physical stimulation—to really feel the sensations in your breasts as they are being kissed and massaged. Concentrating closely on the good feelings can block out all other thoughts and outside distractions. Ellen said that when she experienced her first orgasm, it felt like her clitoris was almost at her chin, she was concentrating on it so hard.

According to Kinsey 36 per cent of the women who masturbated used nothing more than physical stimulation to have an orgasm.[8] If you don't fantasize easily and pornography just doesn't turn you on, try concentrating very carefully on the tactile sensations. Some women enjoy being rubbed with oil, feathers, leather, etc. as a real tactile arousal. The physical stimulation is clearly important for women. For most of us, when the stimulation stops the arousal stops. So we can capitalize on this responsiveness to physical stimulation by really exploring it and focusing on it.

Alcohol and some tranquilizers can have a disinhibiting effect on some women. Evelyn says that having a few glasses of wine before making love not only helps to relax her, but as with other alcoholic drinks, makes her less self-conscious. She becomes more assertive and feels greater freedom to express her sexuality.

Alcohol and tranquilizers are similar in that a small amount can enhance sexuality while a large amount can lower sexual excitability.[9] Too much of either can result in sleep rather than passion and there is no predetermined amount that indicates how much is too much for each individual. Some women can get high on a glass of wine and others don't feel a thing after several glasses of scotch. Through careful experimentation you can find out how much allows you to loosen up and how much pushes you into oblivion.

Many people find that marijuana can also enhance sexuality.[10] It can act to relax inhibitions in much the same way that alcohol does. However, some women have reported that their experience with pot is so concrete and literal that they cannot get beyond the feeling of skin rubbing on skin to enjoy the sexual sensations produced by the skin being rubbed.

You can try some of these aids on your own first with masturbation and then if and when you feel comfortable you can weave them into your shared love-making. Use your imagination. Take a risk and maybe try out some of your secret erotic fantasies or thoughts. As long as your partner is agreeable, no one else need be consulted. Probably the worst outcome would be uproarious laughter and possible disruption of the sexual mood. But with experimentation, you will probably discover things that enhance your sex life and which may even keep you feeling turned on for days.

What we are setting out to do is to free the mind to concentrate on sexual feelings. Putting your body in the right place is the first step. Putting your mind there too completes the picture.

7: *Why Masturbation?*

Masturbation is one of the best ways to learn about your sexual responses. Once you learn about how you respond—through stimulating yourself while free of outside distractions—you will be in a better position to shift your own body movement during love-making to achieve more pleasure or to teach your partner how to stimulate you in the manner that is most likely to lead you to sexual pleasure and eventually to orgasm.

According to Kinsey, "Masturbation may be defined as deliberate self-stimulation which effects sexual arousal."[1] The stimulation can be direct manual stimulation of the genitals or other parts of the body; it can entail the use of objects other than the hand to effect arousal: it can be the result of muscular tension or just psychological stimulation. The stimulation does not have to result in orgasm to be called masturbation.[2]

Of all sexual practices, masturbation is probably the most difficult to talk about. It is an intimate and very personal experience which we have been taught is dirty, sinful, shameful, even physically debilitating. The guilt, fear, anxiety, and repulsion that surrounds masturbation is astounding, especially when one realizes not only how pervasive it is among human beings, but how beneficial, pleasurable, and relaxing an experience it can be. Most importantly, from the standpoint of the pre-orgasmic woman, it is the surest, most effective way to achieve orgasmic release. Many women don't consider the orgasms they have with masturbation as being "real." They believe that "true orgasms" occur only during intercourse. But as was discussed in Chapter 5, all orgasms are real no matter how they are produced, although the total subjective experience may differ depending on the situation and mode of stimulation.

Sixty-two per cent of the women Kinsey interviewed

masturbated, and only 4 to 6 per cent of these women masturbated without reaching orgasm.[3] The ones who did experience orgasm were able to do so in 95 per cent of their masturbatory experiences.[4] Hence, almost all women who masturbate enjoy orgasm through self-stimulation almost every time that they undertake to do so.

Over all, Kinsey found that "the type of premarital activity in which the female had acquired her experience did not appear to have been as important as the fact that she had or had not experienced orgasm."[5] Women who had experienced orgasm premaritally, through any means, were able to respond orgasmically with marital sex three times as often as women who had no orgasmic experience prior to marriage.[6] Masters and Johnson found that the orgasms produced by masturbation occurred more dependably, more rapidly, and were of greater intensity than those achieved through stimulation by a partner.[7] These are just a few of the statistics that support the value of masturbation as an excellent way to go about discovering and learning about your own sexuality, and to achieve orgasm.

The reason self-stimulation works so well to produce orgasm is that you are the only one involved. There is no one else to distract you or for you to worry about pleasing. You can focus totally on yourself, take as much time as you need, and you don't need a partner who is willing to co-operate. You are the one in control, which has benefits. First of all, once you are free from being observed you can focus all your attention on the different kinds of touches, pressures, and positions. The instant feedback of self-stimulation allows you to change things to meet your needs. If the feelings are getting too intense or uncomfortable you can stop for a while, until you become more familiar with those feelings. You never have to go faster than is comfortable. Also, since one's first orgasms are frequently mild in intensity, you are more likely to recognize one when it occurs because orgasms with masturbation tend to be more intense.

If you are uncertain as to whether you have ever experienced orgasm or are certain that you haven't, masturbation can be the key to orgasmic discovery. After her group ended, Sherry said, "I have no doubt that if I hadn't masturbated, I would never have had an orgasm." Once you have learned to overcome your inhibitions and abandon yourself to the physical sensations of orgasm with masturbation you may become more capable of responding in a similar way with your partner—if you want to. The successful experience of having orgasms with masturbation helps to build up positive expectations of having more orgasms by yourself and eventually with a partner. If you choose to continue to hold back the orgasm you can do so, but at least you'll have the choice.

Contrary to popular belief, women do not get "hooked" on masturbation, thereby becoming incapable of having orgasms in any other way. Kinsey states, "We have seen very few cases of females who had encountered any difficulty with transferring their masturbatory experience to coitus, although we have seen some hundreds of cases of females who were considerably disturbed because they were unable to accomplish the anatomic impossibility of transferring their clitoral reactions to vaginal responses."[8]

According to Mary Jane Sherfey, "orgasm tends to increase pelvic vasocongestion; thus, the more orgasms achieved, the more can be achieved."[9] The more orgasms you have by any method—self-stimulation included—the more sexually responsive you are likely to become. The more you exercise and keep the muscles toned, the healthier and better your body systems—including the sexual—will become.

Even if you achieve orgasm frequently there are many good reasons to masturbate. For example, masturbation is always available including times when your partner isn't—either because you are physically separated or because your lover is not in the mood at the same time that you are. Masturbation allows you to be sexually independent from a partner. When your partner is trying to get a good night's sleep, he may find your attempts to arouse him exasperating. Your ability to produce your own orgasm can reduce pressure on your partner to perform. Compare this situation to eating. Sometimes you may be hungry when your partner isn't around; you might prefer to eat with him, but you wouldn't consider starving just so you could eat together. You can satisfy your hunger for food by yourself with a meal or a snack and you can still join your partner later on if you like. This is also true of sexual hunger. Also, there may be times when you don't feel like interacting with your partner, times when you would prefer to be totally self-engrossed, forget the need to respond to him, and enjoy masturbation just for the relaxing satisfaction it provides you. Your mate can also benefit from your self-sufficiency. If you are self-sufficient, both people in the relationship gain more freedom to express their own needs in their own style rather than having to adapt their sexual tempo to that of a partner. And in no way need participation in masturbation be viewed as a reflection on the adequacy of the couple's sexual relationship. Masturbation can enlarge your sex life, not restrict it. Furthermore, masturbation can afford you a sense of control and self-confidence while helping you to like and enjoy your body better. And it's fun—an easy way to feel good all over.

Still, a reasonable proportion of women don't masturbate for a variety of reasons. During the 1800s many books were written by physicians describing the horrors of masturbation. David Cole Gordon, in a small book called *Self Love*,[10] describes the ways in which masturbation was said to be responsible for all the major social and medical ills.

Masturbation was alleged to cause warts on one's hands, hair on the palms of hands, blindness, acne, sterility, and deformed babies. It was deemed responsible for all sorts of psychological problems. The source of this belief is an interesting one. It appears that doctors observed institutionalized mental patients and found that they masturbated. Of course, it should be noted that because these people were institutionalized, no sexual outlet was available other than masturbation. Bizarre as it may sound, these were the observations that led to the conclusion that masturbation was the cause of the lunacy.[11]

Early myths about the physical and psychological dangers of masturbation have been well ingrained. Davis noted that most women who discontinued masturbating did so due to their fear that it would cause mental and physical deterioration.[12] Ann began masturbating as the result of the group treatment program and developed a urinary tract infection. Her immediate reaction was to think that the masturbation had caused it. She asked her doctor (a woman) about it and the doctor replied with a laugh that *she* had never developed a urinary tract infection from masturbating.

Other common reasons that prevent women from masturbating include moral proscription, not being aware that women could do it, or not knowing how to do it.[13] Margaret Mead says, "The female child's genitals are less exposed, subject to less maternal manipulation and less self-manipulation."[14] Therefore, it is likely that female children may fail to discover that their sex organs are sensitive to pleasurable stimulation.

Other obstacles to masturbating stem from the partner and the social situation. Jenny was afraid to masturbate for fear that she would be so turned on by her body that she would only be attracted to other female bodies thereafter and would become a lesbian. Many women feel a sense of self-devaluation if they masturbate, because they assume that a woman resorts to masturbation only if she can't get anything better.

Many men feel threatened by the idea that women masturbate, especially with a vibrator. A man may feel that if his partner can be sexually fulfilled on her own, she will have no need for him. He often does not recognize the previously mentioned advantages that masturbation affords him. What is inferred is that masturbation will lower a woman's desire for sexual contact with a partner. One woman told her male gynecologist that she masturbated and he gently told her that it was bad for her because she was depriving her husband of the pleasure that was his. In reality, a study by Greenberg showed no statistically significant relation between the frequency of masturbation and the frequency of intercourse among the women polled.[15] Most women who masturbate have enough sexual energy to allow for masturbation as well as sexual activity with a partner.

A considerable number of women avoid masturbation because they consider it morally wrong. Several religious denominations have condemned masturbation, sometimes in the context of a broader condemnation of any sexual activity that is not aimed at reproduction, or because it reflects carnal as opposed to spiritual pursuits.[16] These moral grounds have been a prime factor in preventing numerous women from beginning to masturbate.[17] However, once a woman has discovered masturbation as a sexual release, evidence indicates that she will only rarely discontinue the practice because of religious condemnation. Instead, she is likely to continue masturbating while experiencing significant feelings of guilt.[18] Greenberg found that almost half the females who masturbated felt guilty about it.[19] Any possible harmful effects of masturbation come from the worry and concern women have about the abnormality of the activity rather than from the activity itself. According to Kinsey ". . . some millions of the females in the United States, and larger number of males, have had their self-assurance, their social efficiency, and some-

times their sexual adjustments in marriage needlessly damaged—not by their masturbation, but by the conflict between
practice and moral codes. There is no other type of sexual
activity which has worried so many women."[20] We can be
hopeful that feelings of guilt surrounding masturbation have
decreased, at least for younger women, since Kinsey's time.
The Playboy Foundation Study found that 60 per cent of the
women interviewed who were between the ages of eighteen
and twenty-four are currently masturbating as compared to
25 to 30 per cent of Kinsey's sample;[21] in the twenty-six to
thirty-five age group of married adults, about 68 per cent of
the women were continuing the practice even after marriage.[22]

It could hardly be expected that after reading these pas-
sages, you will automatically and magically lose all of the
negative feelings you may have about masturbation. The first
time that you contemplate it you probably won't feel very
comfortable with the idea that self-stimulation is a good thing
for you. But the act itself, and the positive learning about your
sexual self that can be derived may, in time, make you more
comfortable with the idea.

Despite the substantial negative conditioning surrounding
the act of masturbation, Hunt[23] and Kinsey[24] both obtained
figures that showed that 60 to 65 per cent of the women interviewed had masturbated at some time during their lives.
Heterosexual petting is the form of sexual activity the largest
number of females report participating in before marriage;
coitus is the sexual activity most frequently performed after
marriage; and masturbation is the second most common activity that women engage in both before and after marriage.[25]

Females can stimulate themselves sexually in many ways.
Most commonly, female masturbation consists of manipulat-
ing the clitoris, the inner lips, or the whole genital area. Or,
by simply creating pressure by exerting muscular tension of
the thighs and buttocks. Other methods include running water
directly on the clitoris; use of a vibrator, douches, rubbing of
the genitals against pillows, clothing, or other objects. Beth
had always masturbated by exerting rhythmical and steady
muscle pressure while on her stomach with a pillow between
her legs. She could have an orgasm after about twenty seconds, but she was unable to transfer this technique to partner
sex since this position could not be used in love-making with
a partner. She learned to masturbate manually, and then
could experience orgasms with a partner.

Chapter 8 will try to help you discover how to reach orgasm through masturbation. The exercises are important. Chapter 9 is designed to try to help you develop and extend your sexuality with self-stimulation, and set the stage for transferring what you've learned to a partner relationship. Masturbation can be the first step in becoming orgasmic. Not only is it a pleasurable and natural activity, but also it provides effective tools for change which will be used later.

8: Exercises

If you follow the steps in this chapter carefully and closely, chances are excellent that you will be able to become orgasmic within several weeks of practice.

In Chapter 4 we discussed the necessity of setting aside time and a private comfortable space in which to develop your sexuality. Now is the time to do it. You'll have to establish different priorities in your life to make time for yourself. You may even have to give up something different each day of the week in order to find an hour to devote to your sexuality. You'll have to take the time for yourself assertively because if you don't you're likely to find that the day has ended and there is no time left to practice. Days can slip by in this way unless you are determined to make the time for your exercises.

Pick a time when you're not too tired. Marion had difficulty making the time. She would do her sexual homework at one o'clock in the morning just as she was going to bed and would often fall asleep in the middle of practicing. Then she set different priorities. One day, instead of practicing her flute, she practiced her sexual exercises during that hour; another day she got up an hour early and a third day, instead of making the elaborate dinner she had initially planned, she settled for a simple meal instead. During that week she realized that she had been having orgasms during those late night sessions, but she had been too tired to recognize them. I know that if you can take time for yourself, you'll feel better about yourself and others will feel better about you. Someone who is feeling good about herself is much more enjoyable to be around than someone who is always concerned because she is not doing enough. If you have children, feeling better about yourself will result in your being a better companion and model for them.

You will need to practice the exercises. An hour a day, *ev-*

ery day, should be set aside for two to five weeks if you want to re-establish the sexual connections that have been disconnected for all these years.

Once you have made the decision to find an hour each day, think about how you can feel in a more sensual mood. Your mood is important, so pick a time when you are at ease and your energy level is fairly high. Take a long shower or bath; bring some fresh flowers into the room, light some candles, or burn some incense if you like. Or do whatever will create a sensual scene for you. Pretend a lover is returning from a long trip and arrange the room in the kind of romantic setting you know you both would enjoy. Lie down and enjoy the time; one of your favorite lovers can be you.

Learning to express your full sexuality means starting from the beginning. In our culture achieving sexual ease and comfort does not come naturally, any more than learning to walk would if you had spent your early years contained in a small box. In order to learn to walk you would have to get out of the small box and learn to use your legs—crawling, standing, and then finally walking. In order to have orgasmic sexual experiences you may have to learn about sexual stimulation from the beginning, in the comfortable setting you've designed for yourself. Don't rush things. You have lots of time. All you need is practice and determination. You have to begin feeling that you have the right to an orgasm, for yourself, rather than to keep your partner from feeling inadequate as a lover; you deserve the pleasure that a satisfying sexual relationship can bring.

For now, concentrate on learning to have an orgasm on your own through self-stimulation. Later you can concentrate on transferring the orgasm to the partner relationship. Certainly you can continue to make love with your partner as frequently as you usually do, but while you are having sex with him make certain that you *do not* reach orgasm. Don't even think about orgasm; just concentrate on the feelings that you do experience with love-making and leave the orgasm for the hour a day you spend with yourself. If you feel yourself approaching orgasm with your partner, keep yourself from going over the top.

If you have not already done the exercises in Chapters 4 and 5, begin with them. Examine your body thoroughly, visually and through touch, for that first hour. During your hour the next day, examine your genitals with a mirror and explore each area to see if you notice any difference in sensitivity or sensations in the various parts of the genital area. Don't forget the Kegel exercises.

The exercise for the third night is to begin the actual masturbation. You may need to use some oil—massage oil, baby oil, coconut oil, or even vegetable oil will do. Do not use Vaseline; it is not water soluble and can cause problems if it gets in the vagina or urethra. Scented massage oils can add to your sensual experience, but be careful that the oil contains no alcohol, since alcohol can irritate the mucous membranes of the genitals.

Use oil, saliva, or the natural lubrication of the vagina to keep the genital tissues moist so that no irritation develops. Explore by stimulating the area with various types of strokes and pressures. What do very light feathery touches feel like? How about harder rubbing? Try massaging the clitoral area with your fingertips by making gentle but firm circular motions. Some women like to stimulate the glans of the clitoris directly while others find this area too sensitive for direct stimulation and prefer to massage the areas directly surrounding the clitoris above, below, or to the sides. Find out what feels best for you. Many women rub one finger back and forth over the clitoris with varying speeds and intensity. Or the clitoris could be massaged between the forefinger and middle finger, massaging also the whole area by stroking up and down the clitoral shaft. Many women enjoy having their fingers or something else in their vagina while the clitoris is being stroked.

If you notice some irritation of the area, you may be rubbing the skin surface rather than the structures below. A deeper type of rubbing generally produces less irritation to the genitals; rub as though you were massaging a tense muscle and wanted to reach the structures below the skin. This rubbing would be different from the type you would use if you had a skin irritation and were rubbing the surface with a cream. If you do rub too hard or irritate the area, try moving a little more slowly and begin the stimulation with lighter stroking. Don't be concerned; the irritation will disappear within a few hours or a day at the most. It may take a day or two for the genital area to get used to the stimulation.

Remember, you're on a fact-finding mission now. You're learning. Feel whatever there is to feel. Don't hold back in anticipation; don't measure your sensations. Instead, just tune in to any feelings that you do experience and enjoy them. Do you feel any sensations? At first, you will probably feel very little, but continue, and take note of even slight feelings. It is precisely these little feelings which later turn into greater ones, but only after considerable practice.

In our groups we found that women tend to get stymied at various stages in the process of self-stimulation. The most consistent initial difficulty is finding the time to practice. Women try masturbating once or twice for a short period of time and, feeling discouraged and guilty, conclude that there never will be any hope for them, that there must be an easier way—and they give up. Perhaps it's like the first time you tried to bake a cake; it probably burned. If you had never tried again you would have been a failure at cake baking. Perhaps instead you tried several times, went through a few trials before your cake was even edible: but now, it's probably pretty good. If you don't invest some real time in self-sexuality you won't get any results. The time is your responsibility. For most women, getting in contact with their sexuality takes perserverance. Many women require an hour every day for two to five weeks, so if you don't feel anything during the first few days, stick with it. You have lots of time ahead of you.

Some women find that despite their intellectual acceptance of masturbation, self-stimulation produces feelings of disgust, shame, guilt, or embarrassment. Your early negative conditioning about masturbation can reassert itself while you're in the act of doing it. Angela felt very guilty. She would do her exercises in the bedroom where there was a picture of her parents hanging on the wall. She felt as if she were being watched and felt extremely guilty. Finally she turned the picture around and subsequently felt a whole lot better. Abby first did the exercises under the covers because she was embarrassed. Sarah used a blindfold—and had her first orgasm. Janice was uncomfortable with the homework, but felt reassured when she told her husband prior to beginning the assignment, "At least I know there are five other gals in the Bay Area doing what I'm going to do tonight." The five others were in her group. You can be assured that there are many more than five other females masturbating at any given time in your town. Kelly's initial reaction was that it was bad and dirty to be touching her genitals with her hand, but she got over the feelings with time and practice as did Carmen, who responded to the exercise assignment by asking us if we were sure there wasn't some other way for her to become orgasmic. At first, she didn't want to do the exercises, but after other women began reporting that they were feeling sensations they had never felt before—and after one woman had an orgasm—Carmen decided it might be good training. By the time the group had ended, Carmen was orgasmic and masturbation for its own sake was more than acceptable to her.

If you're still finding masturbation and the thought of it disagreeable and offensive, don't try to fight the feelings. Exaggerate them! While you are stimulating yourself, let yourself feel disgusted. Make disagreeable sounds and exaggerate the motions that offend you. Stay with the foolish or uncomfortable feelings. Exaggerating them for a couple of hours should help to neutralize your negative feelings about the exercise.

Another difficulty that may arise for many women is that they say they feel *nothing*, even after a number of days of consistent practice. If you are one of these women, let's compare with your expectations the feelings you label as "nothing." Are you really feeling nothing? Or are you just not feeling what you anticipated? Compare the feeling in your clitoris to that in your elbow. Any difference? A small difference? Good! Keep at it. Maybe you are expecting to experience something different from the feelings that you are experiencing at this time. However, by constantly focusing on what is *not* there, you may be losing sight of the feelings that *do* exist for you. A good strategy is to concentrate on what *is* happening rather than on what is not happening. At the beginning, you are looking for information about yourself—*not* instant orgasm. Even negative information—discovering the things that don't turn you on—is important.

Involve other parts of your body in addition to your genitals in the sexual stimulation. Massage your inner thighs, breasts or nipples, or other erotically sensitive areas with one hand as you stimulate the genital area with the other. Stimulate any sensitive area in the manner that feels best to you. You, and you alone, know what is most exciting and pleasurable to you. You are engaged in becoming the expert on yourself so explore a bit until you discover what feels best.

Don't forget the mental aphrodisiacs. Erotic writings, pictures or films, and fantasy can held take your mind off the cares of the day and focus it on the sensual feelings. Edna had her first orgasm after returning from seeing her first pornographic movie. Many women enjoy the "most patient lover" fantasy. Pretend that you are making love and your lover is infinitely patient. Your lover is willing to do anything and everything for you. A second enjoyable fantasy might be to imagine yourself as the world's most sensuous woman who is teaching an inexperienced lover the art of pleasing a woman.

Using muscular tension by rhythmically contracting the muscles in the pelvic and thigh region, or doing the Kegels while stimulating the clitoral area manually can enhance your pleasure. A glass of wine or a martini might relax you for your hour so that you are better able to concentrate on the good feelings. If you find that your mind wanders while you are masturbating, take some time off to think about various nonerotic things We all need some time to daydream, so acknowledge that need Spend fifteen minutes just letting your imagination roam freely and you may find that after that time you are more ready to attune your mind to sexual, sensual thoughts.

Let yourself go. Experiment. Darlene found it a turn-on to do the exercises while partially clothed. She said she felt like a dancer in a burlesque show and the thought really enhanced her sexual mood. Also, remember that music may either enhance arousal, or it can interfere with it.

To reach orgasm takes practice and time and the right mental attitude Without the support of a group working together on the problem it might be a little more difficult, but don't get discouraged If you feel as though you don't want to go on, then take a break. Many people find the exercises really enjoyable, so if you're finding them a chore or if you're spending the time but hating it, discontinue them for a day or two. Then resume the exercises when the pressure is off. Katie was really discouraged. She came to the group crying and just about ready to give up. She had only experienced two small sensations over the previous days of homework and she wasn't even sure that she knew where her clitoris was. We told her to stimulate herself using a mirror so she could see where she was touching. It was clear that she was trying too hard and not enjoying it enough. She was looking for headlines and not paying enough attention to the fine print. Four days later she arrived exuberant, having discovered her first orgasm. After the group ended, Katie offered to come into other groups and tell them about her success story. She was

twenty-six years old and had never had a single sexual feeling
in her life. Now she was having orgasms and couldn't believe
it.

You might find that without the aid of group support to
make you stick with it, it's likely that you will find all sorts of
ways to procrastinate. Here are some of the common problems I have heard from the women in the groups, and also
ways to solve them. Perhaps by recognizing them you can
devise ways to get beyond the early natural resistance. If
you've never masturbated before, your natural urges have
probably been blocked by factors in your background. Overcoming these factors means sticking with the exercises even
though you may find the task difficult at the beginning.

Evelyn complained that her hand got tired, so we suggested
more movement of the fingers and less of the whole arm or
vice versa depending upon the muscles which were being affected. If this problem persists, cut the exercise time down to
half an hour and add five minutes to your time with each succeeding day until you are spending the full hour. It's very common for women to require an hour or even two hours of
stimulation before that first orgasm occurs. Having an orgasm
is like learning a new dance. If you don't get it right the first
time and give up, you'll never learn. It takes time and practice.

Margaret would do the exercises for fifteen seconds while
reading pornography and then would get so involved in the
reading that she would forget about the manual stimulation.
Remember that discontinuing the physical stimulation in females usually lowers the level of sexual arousal. To experience your first orgasm it is important to keep your level of
physical arousal high.

If this process is going to work, you have to really want
the orgasm. If you don't think it worth the effort or if
you don't expect results, you will probably be the victim of a
self-fulfilling prophecy. Because you don't really try, it will
fail. Things won't have changed and you still won't be orgasmic. But what would happen if you *really* tried? Cindy
procrastinated by saying that since she had learned the information now, she would work on it later. "But when is later?"
I asked her. She could have put it off forever without doing
anything about it unless she set some goals right then. She
began to see my point, but having that first orgasm was still a
scary prospect for her. However, she thought it was worth it,
and in the long run she recognized her fear and confronted

it. Eve realized that setting aside time was really important although she had difficulty making an hour's space for herself. She found it took her an hour just to get aroused at all. If she spent less time, she didn't seem to get anywhere.

One of the group leaders, Ms. Jeremy Brav, told a wonderful story as the women sat in a circle and talked about their experiences with the homework exercises. "Sometimes," she said, "I feel like we are all Indian ladies sitting around the campfire. We are trying to figure out how to allow the Great Spirit of the Orgasm to visit us. We can't *make* the Spirit come; it will come of its own accord. But through the years, lore has been handed down and we pass it around while we're waiting. Try this. Well, maybe this will make it come. And lo and behold the lore must work because the Great Spirit of the Orgasm does descend to grace us."

If you've been practicing the exercises for an hour a day for about ten days to two weeks and still aren't getting aroused (I don't mean not having orgasms, I mean not having any sexual feelings at all), there are some nonmanual techniques that may be just what you need to awaken your sexual feelings. I don't recommend using these techniques at the outset because I've found that it is better for women to touch themselves directly, to become comfortable with the genital area and get used to their bodies and their sexual feelings. In the long run, directly confronting the negative and guilty feelings that arise can make us much more relaxed and at ease with sex.

A good compromise would be to use a vibrator or the running water technique as an addition to manual masturbation. It might make good sense to begin with manual stimulation and then after about ten to fifteen minutes employ another technique. Or, use one method one day and another the next day.

Many children discover the running water or bathtub technique. It consists of lying in the tub and maneuvering your body so that the genitals are directly under the faucet (this may not be physically possible given the shape of your body and the design of your tub); or attach a small hose to the faucet. Direct the stream of warm water onto the clitoral area. The sensation produced is akin to that of a thousand tiny fingers rapidly moving over the genitals. The pressure of the water on this sexually sensitive area can produce an orgasm. I say "can" because, as with other types of stimulation, it is possible to fight the orgasm and prohibit it from happening, despite the effectiveness of the physical stimulation. I shall discuss this process in greater detail later. The best thing to do is to get used to the sensations gradually. Stay under the water for a while and then move away when you begin feeling some sensations that are unfamiliar to you. Then move under again as you gradually become more comfortable with these new feelings. Leslie began experiencing orgasms this way and used to joke about how shriveled her skin was getting from taking so many baths.

Another popular alternate technique is to use one of the many types of vibrator/massagers available at most drug and department stores. They can also be ordered by mail.[1] An electric one is generally preferable. The inexpensive battery operated massagers are fine for some women, but many complain that they are noisier than the electric ones. Heating elements do not seem to be important, but a massager equipped with a variety of attachments can afford the versatility required for individual preferences. The small ball-shaped attachment appears to be a favorite among many women. Again, choice here is totally individual. Some women prefer a gentle vibrator while others like a heavier, more intense machine. If the sensation is too strong, use a towel or some clothing between your body and the vibrator to soften the intensity. When Janice found the sensations produced by the vibrator to be too intense, she would move it elsewhere around her body and then back to her genitals again after a few moments. Experience with the vibrator resulted in her remarking, "Sex is more physical than I gave it credit for."

Some women are hesitant to use a vibrator for fear that they will get "hooked" on it and not be able to have orgasms any other way. First of all, if you haven't been experiencing orgasm any other way, using a vibrator surely can do no harm, especially since there is an excellent chance that you'll become orgasmic this way. Secondly, there is no evidence that women who have orgasms with vibrators are unable to have orgasms with other kinds of stimulation. However, stimulation produced by using water or a vibrator is significantly different from other forms of stimulation, so women who may be orgasmic easily with a vibrator may have to spend more time when other types of stimulation are used. A vibrator sometimes stimulates the urethra, which may result in unintentional urination, but this should cause no alarm. If this should happen to you, practice the Kegel exercises. Urinate before using the vibrator and put a towel on the bed if it makes you feel more secure. But really, why should we be so concerned over expelling a few drops of urine? A vibrator may be equivalent to using training wheels to learn to ride a bicycle. You get the feeling of what the experience is like and then, if you want to, you can practice without the machine. However, there is no reason to stop using a vibrator, either alone or with a partner, if you enjoy it. Many women have very successfully integrated the vibrator into their sexual relationship with a partner before, during, after, or instead of intercourse. Some men enjoy the sensation of the vibrator on their body and genitals too.

If the masturbation is working and you are beginning to feel new and different sexual feelings, you may find this as upsetting as not feeling any sensations at all. Angela found that the more she became interested in sex and enjoyed it, the more guilty she felt. As we feel more, it seems that the old sexual taboos come back to haunt us. We think we have gotten over the guilt and fears, and then they show up again to plague us once more: Maybe we really will lose consciousness or become a nymphomaniac. Let the fears come. Exaggerate them! What is your worst fantasy? That you'll sleep with every man in town and that your telephone number will be found on the walls of men's rooms? Let your fears take over, follow them to their limit—no matter how absurd they become. Trying to ignore the fears and pretend that they aren't there often requires more energy than giving them full rein. Reality is rarely as bad as your worst fears.

Karen McLellan, who leads pre-orgasmic women's groups in Berkeley, talks about a lesson she has learned from T'ai Chi: "If something's coming at you (your fears, for example) and you try to force that thing back, then it ultimately gets you. At the very least, all your energy is wasted holding it at bay. So I say, when your bad feelings come in, don't try to force them away. Let them come; and then say, 'Oh, it's just that stuff again. Oh yes, I know you. So long, I'm doing something else now; I'll get to you later.' "

As you masturbate, let the fears come. Try to make them bigger; then smaller. Have fun changing the size and intensity of the fears. Play with them and let them wash over you like waves. Getting to know them well can keep them from seeming so overwhelming, so scary, and can keep them from interfering with your sexual progress.

Some women experience intense feelings when they first begin the masturbation assignments and then suddenly feel nothing during successive efforts. If this happens to you, don't worry—if you could feel the sensations once, you can feel them again. More than likely, the intensity of the initial sensations frightened you and caused you to hold back. Discontinue the masturbation for a few days and then very slowly begin again.

Become familiar with your new sexual feelings. You don't have to discover the whole range of feelings in one day or even one week. Move on slowly and push a little bit further ahead each time. It's like going out on a branch for an apple. You can creep out a bit, then move back some to where it feels safer; then creep out just a tiny bit more, then back again, and then another tiny move out. Soon you'll feel safe at the beginning of the branch and only frightened when you get out toward the end near the apple. Little by little, with continuous testing, you'll slowly begin to feel safe with the new sensations. You'll learn to trust yourself and the branch. You won't lose control and fall. The branch remains stable and the apple is almost within reach.

Getting close to orgasm often feels like a sneeze that doesn't quite happen. Frequently, reaching these high levels of excitement without release can be as irritating and frustrating as that lost sneeze. The women with whom I work call these levels of excitation "plateaus." All the excitement and sexual tension is there, but they just can't find a way to move beyond to orgasm. After a number of sessions that stop at this plateau, women can become quite demoralized and discouraged.

The responsibility for overcoming this last barrier to reaching orgasm is primarily yours. Try to push beyond this point by stimulating yourself a few seconds beyond the time when you would ordinarily stop. With each succeeding session, continue the stimulation until you reach a level of slightly higher intensity before stopping. Sometimes the feelings will build and at other times they will diminish. Just at the point you may think that you've lost them forever, they may suddenly return.

If you are stuck at the high plateau level but have not

succeeded in going over it to experience the release of orgasm, you're probably expending as much energy fighting the orgasm as you are trying to make it happen. Relax, but don't stop the stimulation. There is one kind of muscular tension that fights the orgasm and another kind that enhances it. If you feel your whole body becoming a tightened spring, try to relax, but continue to stimulate the genital area. Breathe deeply; imagine the air being breathed in and out of your vagina, rather than your mouth. This helps to ease the anxiety. Change positions to eliminate some of the excess tension. If breathing deeply and regularly doesn't work, maybe you need to hold your breath. Lydia found that holding her breath helped her get over the plateau stage while Sally experienced just the opposite. Experiment with several different breathing patterns to see what works for you; for example some women prefer panting in short rhythmic gasps. If you are becoming extremely frustrated, get up and take a thirty-second walk; look out the window. One of the women in the group would get up and brush her teeth when she felt stuck. Stopping won't cause you to lose the feelings completely. They'll return when you start to stimulate yourself again.

Building up sexual tension, letting it ebb and then increasing it again, can produce a level of arousal that some women experience as frightening. Some women fear that the release won't be great enough for the tension that has been built up. Or, that the release will be too great. How can you be sure that you won't explode or disintegrate if all that tension is released? Intellectually, you may know that you won't, but the intensity of the feelings could make you hold back.

The experience of reaching the plateau and not being able to get over reminds me of a similar situation I encountered while learning rock climbing. To descend over a steep face, the rock climber must use a rope fastened around his or her backside at one end and attached to a tree or another climber at the other end. This process is called rappelling. A good friend and I were atop a forty-foot sheer face where she was teaching me how to rappel. I turned my back to the edge and took a timid step backward. The objective was to step backward off the ledge and lower myself slowly, using the rope for support. I knew all this intellectually but I still had to take that last step backward over the edge. I became more and more frightened. I took a few deep breaths. I walked forward and stopped, then stepped slowly backward to the edge of the cliff, unable to step off. I repeated this process a dozen times without going over, despite valid assurances that it was absolutely safe. After the twelfth time, I finally decided in my own head that I would have to force myself to step off the cliff into the abyss. So, I took a deep breath, relaxed my body, and stepped off, feeling totally panicked for one split second as I weightlessly dropped over the edge of the tiny distance before the support of the rope securely held me and I began to lower myself down. It became progressively easier each time I had to step off the edge until, after a while, I could rappel with no difficulty whatsoever. The type of determination required to go over the edge of the cliff is similar to that required to have an orgasm. Despite what anyone says, you may still experience that split second of fear. "Will I really fall into nothingness?" you may ask. The only way to convince yourself you'll survive is to relax, let go, and see what happens. But passing through that fear will bring you to the other side. Both the pleasure of the experience and the attainment of the goal are worth the risk.

The turning point for Carmen came when she remembered what Katie had told her. After Katie had experienced her first orgasm she said to Carmen, "If you *want* it to work, it *does* work. It will happen if you just let go." In order for Judy to have an orgasm she imagined the whole group saying, "It's OK, Judy." Carol became orgasmic when she decided *not* to stop the pleasurable feelings although she wasn't expecting to have an orgasm.

Evelyn had an orgasm after deciding she couldn't control other things in her life, especially her financial problems. So she put all her energy into attempting to solve her sexual problem and she had two orgasms that day!

If old fears and concerns return they can be combatted. Cindy borrowed a friend's vibrator. While her children were too busy watching TV to interrupt her, she spent two and a half hours masturbating but had her first orgasm within the first hour. After it was over, she wondered if she had really had one. She said, "I had this tickly sensation. My body was lifting up and I was trying to get more sensation. I was moving my body around and my nipples became erect. Then came this scared feeling I always had, but I stuck with it and it went away. I held my breath and felt really good, giggly; warm. It was fast. The tickly sensation came, I let go, and felt fine again. I tried breathing and this intensified the feeling. There was no pressure; I wanted to spend the afternoon doing it. Eventually I continued without the vibrator."

Some women find that it helps if they role-play. When they reach a plateau, they move their body around as if they were having an orgasm. Exaggerate the pretend orgasm. Act as if it were very intense. Make lots of sounds and exaggerate the body movements. Sarah did this and to her surprise a real orgasm followed soon after the simulated one.

Don't give up, but if you feel discouraged and frustrated don't pretend that those feelings don't exist either. Rather, attempt to get in deeper touch with them. Allow your whole body to feel discouraged. Consider the possibility that you may never allow yourself to take that final leap, because only you can do it for yourself. Janice was very discouraged and I told her to get in touch with the fact that she might never have an orgasm. I told her to go home and really think about that possibility. This really made her angry. She said, "Why should I get in touch with never having an orgasm? I've been in touch with that for thirty years. I'm not going to think about that. I'm going to have it if it kills me!" And she did— the very next day.

Don't forget about experimenting with the expression of other feelings too if you have a tendency to keep everything, including sexual feelings, safely locked inside. Holding emotions inside requires a tremendous amount of energy, energy that could be better used in being creative, productive, feeling intimate and sexual. Experiment for a week or two. Allow your feelings to "hang out" for that length of time by expressing the feelings as soon as you feel them. If you tend to cover things over with a smile it may be especially important to practice expressing feelings. Ellen had a fight with her husband. It was the first time she had expressed her angry feelings in a long time. She did the exercises that night and had her first orgasm. She said it measured 10 on the Richter scale.

In general, however, first orgasms are not very intense. They take a long time to achieve and may be barely noticeable. Sometimes women are disappointed after all the work and effort. The lack of intensity in the beginning frequently results from the amount of energy invested in fighting the orgasm. As you experience more orgasms and become less afraid and anxious, the orgasms can become more intense.

Some women prefer mild orgasms. Kelly had mild orgasms and had no desire to intensify the experience.

After experiencing the first orgasm, many women become afraid that they won't be able to have another one. Frequently, they repeat the exercises immediately to see if it can happen again. After one orgasm, Laurie kept masturbating over and over again to make sure it was really true. Sherry recreated the exact scene to insure that the orgasm would be repeated. Women are afraid that the new-found skill will disappear unless they follow the magical method that caused it to occur the first time. It takes a while before you can be comfortable and assured that orgasm will occur. Most of the time it will. Occasionally it won't so don't worry, it's not lost. You may have to relax a bit more, or be more in the mood.

Sometimes the orgasm doesn't come simply because you're trying to force it to happen. It seems that when the pressure is turned on, the orgasm is turned off. Laurie found it helped to be able just to enjoy the feelings without having to reach an orgasm. Inevitably, when she could relax and just feel good with no goal in mind, the orgasm would occur. Sexual sensations ebb and flow. You may feel turned on, and then lose the feeling. There is no need to struggle for the lost sensation as another one will develop soon if you relax. Sexual feelings are like waves in the ocean. There is no need to break your neck to keep riding a particular wave when you can relax and wait to catch another one. There are an infinite number of waves in the sea.

First, learn to be comfortable about having orgasms on your own. Then, you can try to integrate them into your love-making with your partner—if you want to. Sherry found that she really needed to experience orgasm by herself awhile before she was ready to share it with her partner. Nina, on the other hand, was orgasmic with her husband almost as soon as she was by herself. Every woman is different. Check and see how you feel and what is comfortable for you now.

Leslie's husband was upset because he said sex wasn't any better for him even though she had become orgasmic. This put her under pressure to have her orgasms for his pleasure and not for herself. She finally got up the nerve to set him straight. She had waited forty-eight years to be orgasmic and now he could wait to share them.

Once you are experiencing orgasms with masturbation you may find at first that sex with your partner can be disappointing. This is not uncommon. Polly became comfortable with masturbation, and enjoyed the orgasms which resulted, but she felt frustrated by love-making with her partner because she could not attain the same release. Soon, however, when the novelty of the masturbation wore off, Polly renewed her interest in partner sex again. Janice was just the opposite. Before she entered the group she avoided sex whenever possible, but once she began having orgasms with masturbation, her attitude toward sex changed. She wasn't having orgasms with her partner yet, but she was enjoying sex; her whole attitude was more positive.

Whether or not you are orgasmic with your partner, there is no reason to stop masturbating. Instead of looking at self-stimulation from an antiquated perspective—as a substitute for the "real thing"—why not view it as one of many alternative forms of sexual expression—provided by nature for a party of one.

9: *Elaborating on What You've Learned*

If you have recently learned to masturbate or even if you have been orgasmic with masturbation through most of your life, you may not find yourself totally comfortable with the experience. In my first pre-orgasmic women's group I set out to advocate masturbation to other women even though I was not as yet totally comfortable with the idea myself. However, through the course of my work, this feeling changed. My experience demonstrates that it is possible to learn about one's sexuality through self-stimulation without first being completely at ease with the idea. Comfort with masturbation may come with time and positive experience.

One way to begin exploring self-stimulation further is by making it a new and different experience. Experiment by doing something new, something you've never tried before. Carol experimented by stroking her body with feathers, silk, leather, and other textured materials before and during masturbation.

Many women have a tendency to remain dissatisfied. In the therapy program, women sometimes argue that orgasms with masturbation are not "real" or worthwhile. Women who are orgasmic may complain because they are not *multi*-orgasmic. Others who are multi-orgasmic may complain that their orgasms aren't intense enough. Those who have to fantasize to achieve orgasm may label themselves abnormal. Those who don't fantasize may feel that they are missing out. One way or another, people can find ways to negate their experiences if they want to.

If you would like to intensify your orgasmic experiences somewhat or experience multiple orgasms, there are techniques that might enable you to do so. You can experiment with these and see if you like the results, or if you prefer your original pattern.

The most effective way to intensify an orgasm is by prolonging the pleasurable experience preceding it through a process called "teasing." First, build genital tension and maintain it at a peak but don't let yourself get excited enough to reach orgasm. Stimulate yourself a bit, enough to get closer but not too close to orgasm, and then change the site of stimulation to an area that is less sensitive. Or use a lighter, more delicate, teasing touch. Feel the level of arousal rise and drop, then hang suspended. Take your time, enjoy the feelings. Keep up the teasing for a while before intensifying the stimulation enough to trigger the orgasm. Teasing allows for a greater build-up of sexual tension, and the more tension that is built up, the greater the orgasmic release. Instead of fighting the pleasure, ride it like a wave—submerged and synchronized. If you relax and flow with the feelings a more intense orgasm should result. *Consciously* relax. Use some deep breathing techniques.[1] (For example, close your eyes and imagine that there is a screen directly in front of your eyes. Focus on the screen and let any images that appear pass through or bounce off the screen. Meanwhile breathe in deeply through your mouth. Then close your mouth and as you exhale, imagine you are actually breathing the air out through the vagina.) Prolonging and flowing freely with the feelings is the key to a more intense response.

Miscalculation can result in a disappointing experience. Betty employed the teasing technique, but when she built up the tension for the third time, she misjudged her level of arousal and accidentally stimulated herself to orgasm. Not being prepared for it, she experienced almost no satisfaction or release.

Another way to intensify orgasms is through exaggeration. Many women keep their bodies totally passive while stimulating the genital area. This may create a split between the active sexual self and the passive, resisting self. Stimulate other erotically sensitive areas in addition to the genitals. Getting your whole body into the sexually active state can enhance the sexual experience. Ellen exaggerated everything. She moved her body more, made more sounds, breathed more deeply, and created more muscular tension. The result lived up to her expectations—a more intense orgasm and a greater sense of release and accompanying relaxation.

Making sounds is often difficult for men as well as women. It is almost as if in the heat of passion we are still attempting to look dignified. Constantly and painfully aware of how others are responding to us, we remain carefully quiet. Withholding noises during sex can have a stifling effect on orgasm. You may not naturally feel like making sounds, and that is fine, but if you are carefully guarding against any escaping sounds, you are not as free to let go completely. Sally's orgasms really began to change when she felt the freedom to express outwardly what she felt inwardly both in terms of noises and body movements.

If you would like to experience multiple orgasms or a slightly different type of orgasmic pattern, you might want to try a vibrator/massager. Vibrators provide a consistent intensity that cannot be duplicated manually. As a result, the stimulation provided by a vibrator may be sufficient to bring you to orgasm one or more times with minimal effort on your part.

Orgasms with vibrators may differ in some respects from those produced by other kinds of stimulation. The build-up with a vibrator may be very brief, in fact, some women find it too brief to achieve the release desired. Other women like the vibrator precisely because it takes so little time and energy. A number of women say that an orgasm with a vibrator feels like an electrical charge coursing through their body. These are women who prefer the slower, more gradual build-up and release provided by manual stimulation.

Vibrators can be enjoyable additions to solo or shared sexual experiences. However, some women who object to the technological computer-instant-freeze-dried orientation of society may classify vibrators with frozen TV dinners, tape-recorded answering services, and microwave ovens. These women generally prefer a return to the more natural, slower, less complicated human functions. Thus, philosophically, they might be unwilling to use a vibrator.

Other women may express the fear that they will turn into a "vibrator junkie" and never be satisfied sexually by any other method of stimulation. To date, this has not been found to be the case. However, some women do tend to get spoiled by the rapidity with which they experience orgasm with a vibrator and may become discouraged with the slower process of having orgasms with manual stimulation. Switching from vibrator to manual stimulation may mean investing more time in masturbation, but you can probably make the switch if you have an interest in doing so. Harriet experienced her first orgasm with a vibrator and continued to use it both alone and with her partner. After six months she decided to try reaching orgasm manually; it was like learning to have an orgasm again for the first time. It took her several days of doing the exercises before, after forty minutes of manual stimulation, she finally had her first orgasm without a vibrator. She was elated because she had almost lost hope of succeeding.

One way that might make the transition from vibrator to manual stimulation easier is to use the vibrator until you experience a high level of arousal and then switch to manual stimulation for reaching the orgasm. The following time, discontinue use of the vibrator at a slightly lower level of arousal. Continue this process until you find that you are able to begin the self-stimulation without use of the vibrator.

Various vibrator substitutes have been reported by women in the groups. And, of course, the sensations produced by the running water technique are similar to those produced by a vibrator. A statement by Phyllis Lyon and Del Martin in *Lesbian Woman* aptly makes the distinction between the physiological and psychological aspects of orgasm. "As Masters and Johnson so well argued, an orgasm is an orgasm, no matter how it is achieved the body goes through the same physiological pattern, whether orgasm comes through a loved one or a vibrating washing machine. The 'quality' of the orgasm differs—not within the body, but within the head. There is, after all, a great deal of difference psychologically between your lover and your washing machine."[2] However, this does not mean that you can't enjoy them both. The only way to find out is to try it.

In order to explore the range of your responsivity and to begin training yourself to experience orgasms with lovemaking, it may be necessary for you to try a variety of positions which resemble positions used with a partner. Many women use only one technique to masturbate and this is the way they have learned to respond orgasmically. Often, this technique or position is not readily adaptable to partner sex, in which case it may be necessary to learn new techniques which are more applicable to partner experiences. Learning to respond with other techniques and positions requires a bit of experimentation. Explore different positions. If you've been lying on your back, bring your knees up to your chest. Try lying on your stomach or in a kneeling position as if there were a partner beneath you. Gradually change the focal point and type of self-stimulation so that it approaches techniques used by a partner. Sensitize your clitoral area to the subtler stimulation resulting from intercourse by lightly stroking this area for twenty minutes a day over a period of about two weeks.

In preparation for orgasms with a partner, practice increasing the sensitivity of the vagina by inserting your fingers or other phallic-shaped objects which will not splinter, cut, or in other ways injure the tissues. Kinsey found that 20 per cent of the masturbating females reported using vaginal insertions some of the time to provide vaginal stimulation while the clitoral area was stimulated manually or mechanically.[8] Although terribly embarrassed, Diane finally disclosed to the group that she had been masturbating by moving a perfume bottle in and out of her vagina. She found this experience very stimulating, and, with the aid of fantasy, one which closely resembled the sensation of intercourse. However, she began to notice a vague burning sensation in her vagina and thought it best to discontinue using the bottle. Since that time she has continued to use other, safer dildoes to enhance her masturbation.

Compare your sensations while with a partner to those you feel when you stimulate yourself while alone. Can you begin to identify when you are turning off or discern what is lacking? Remember, that while the experience of orgasm with masturbation may be psychologically different from an orgasmic experience with your partner, physiologically it is the same. However, some attitudes or skills may be preventing you from utilizing the common elements of the two experiences, and transfering the experience of orgasm to sex with a partner.

10: Rethinking Sexual Goals

Myths and misinformation are major obstacles to enjoying
sex fully and becoming orgasmic with a partner. The following myths have been mentioned earlier in the book, but will
be repeated here because they often play a significant part in
circumscribing our sexual activities and shaping our notions
of what is considered "normal" sexual behavior.

The first myth, and the one that is the most difficult to dispel, is that the so-called "vaginal orgasm" is somehow superior. I hope the information in this book and others has
finally put an end to that myth.[1] A woman who needs more
clitoral stimulation than that indirectly provided by the thrusting of the penis to achieve orgasm is no more abnormal than
a man who requires very rapid thrusting to achieve his climax.

Recent research indicates that most women, although not
all, require some amount of direct clitoral stimulation, just as
most men require some direct penile stimulation, in order to
have an orgasm. About one quarter of the women who completed the group therapy program could achieve orgasm
through intercourse alone, at least occasionally, while two
thirds were able to achieve orgasm if clitoral stimulation accompanied intercourse. Results of a questionnaire in an article by Suzanne White in *Forum Magazine* reveal even higher
figures. Only one fifth of the self-elected respondents found
penile-vaginal thrusting sufficient to achieve orgasm while
three fifths of the sample needed a combination of clitoral
and vaginal stimulation and one fifth required clitoral stimulation alone.[2]

A friend of mine was involved with a woman he liked very
much but was disturbed because she didn't reach orgasm. Finally he asked her if she could have orgasms by herself if she
masturbated. She was taken aback by the question but finally
admitted that she could. He asked her to touch herself the
same way she did when she was by herself, while they had intercourse. It took quite a while the first time, but finally she

did have an orgasm. It was her first with a partner. She was so delighted that her pleasure overcame her embarrassment.

Some women can have orgasms solely through intercourse with certain men and not others. Relationship problems aside, this may occur because of a man's particular rhythm of thrusting or the shape of his pubic bone which allows for greater clitoral stimulation. Is this woman abnormal with one partner and normal with the other? Should she end the relationship with a man she loves or finds compatible simply because in order for her to reach orgasm, their love-making must include other modes of stimulation in addition to intercouse? No. It's absurd that so much emphasis is placed on the manner in which an orgasm is achieved rather than the enjoyment two people derive from their love-making. Nina could have orgasms with intercourse plus clitoral stimulation, but wouldn't let herself accept them as valid. She kept repeating the myth that it wasn't good enough to reach orgasm that way since that wasn't the *right* way.

Some women say that orgasms achieved through vaginal thrusting are "different" or "more satisfying." If you don't have orgasms this way, you may assume this is true and that you are missing something. Having a penis contained within the vagina may enhance sexual pleasure before and during orgasm, but this doesn't preclude the addition of direct clitoral stimulation.

Why not do away with the myth that there are better and worse ways of having an orgasm. Instead, acknowledge that having orgasms through intercourse without additional stimulation may not be possible given your unique physiological make up or the anatomic fit with your partner which may make sufficient clitoral stimulation impossible.

If someone came to you desiring to learn to fly but refusing to use any props to help her, you would be likely to think her absurd; she *might* succeed, but it would be highly improbable. If, however, she would use a glider or some paraphernalia designed specifically to assist in flying, she would probably succeed. She might struggle for years without additional equipment and never succeed, but with proper aids she might fly and enjoy the experience. Apply this analogy to attaining orgasm. You might succeed without clitoral stimulation, but, with it you have a much better chance. The pleasure of the orgasm is the same either way—so why make things difficult for yourself?

The second myth is that sex and intercourse are synonymous; that all sexual encounters must include or culminate in intercourse and orgasm must occur during intercourse; that anything else would not be considered "normal." However, intercourse is only one of a number of ways to give and receive sexual pleasure. Sexual relationships and sexual feelings extend far beyond the act of intercourse. To make intercourse the goal of sex does a grave disservice to many enjoyable ways of touching. It somehow implies that other sexual activities don't really count or aren't really important. It's as though we were really turned on by kissing but would not allow ourselves the option of exploring kissing as a full sexual experience because of an unspoken rule that erotic kissing *must* lead to intercourse.

The term sex includes anything that turns you on and gives you sexual pleasure. It doesn't have to include a partner, but it can. It doesn't have to include orgasm, but that's a possibility. It doesn't even have to include any genital touching—it could just be fantasy. The feelings can last for hours or pass in a flash. You can write your own scripts for each sexual experience and each one may be different. But most importantly, it doesn't *have* to end in intercourse. Other modes of sexual stimulation can comprise a complete sexual experience or intercourse can be enjoyable as foreplay or afterplay.

Another overrated myth is the superiority of the simultaneous orgasm. Both people "should" climax together in one glorious mind-bending explosion. Striving for a simultaneous orgasm can require considerable concentration on what your lover is experiencing and less concentration on and enjoyment of your own experience. Achieving a simultaneous orgasm requires a lot of carefully controlled strategy as opposed to free abandon. "Is he almost there? How fast is he breathing? He's almost there and I'm not; what'll I do?" These thoughts alone can block an individual orgasm, much less a simultaneous one. You may find it more enjoyable for you and your partner to experience consecutive orgasms; in this way you can concentrate totally on your own sexual build-up and release and then concentrate totally on pleasuring your partner and experiencing your partner's excitement and release and vice versa. If you experience simultaneous orgasm, fine; that can be one kind of experience, but not necessarily one to strive for each time. Kelly prefers having consecutive orgasms because then she can relate more to her partner. She said that if they have orgasms at the same time, they both feel more isolated because they are so involved in their own pleasure. Ann said she prefers to have her orgasm first. Then she can better enjoy pleasuring her lover because she feels satisfied, and close to him. Other women like their partners to climax first because then they feel that they can finally relax and become immersed in the sexual feelings. Finding patterns that fit for you with as much or as little variation as you desire is important.

Another important myth to dispel is the belief that the male must be aggressive and the female passive; that it is unfeminine to be sexually assertive and unmasculine to remain passive sexually. If we accept this belief, we prevent the woman from being innovative and expressing her needs and desires and prohibit the man from being able to relax and enjoy being pleasured.

Opening up the relationship to sexual changes initiated by you can pave the way for vast improvements. Since we have been taught that we should not enjoy sex or be sexually aggressive, many women take a very passive role in love-making, expecting their partner to initiate while they remain passively receptive. Sex becomes a dance where the male leads and the female follows. The dance may become routine since the male partner only knows a limited number of steps. Dancing (and sex) could be twice as interesting if the female would also initiate and add steps of her own. Most males enjoy the opportunity of having a partner assume some responsibility for sexual initiation and innovation.[3] It takes some of the burden off them. According to Moulton, "The woman who feels free to be physically active in love-making usually makes a more exciting partner than one who never expresses her own erotic preferences or who takes no initiative, feeling that her role is merely to follow and please the man. This may be gratifying to some men initially, but it is apt to become stereotyped and lifeless to both partners."[4]

Being able to assert yourself is essential because no one can read your mind. You are going to have to take the initiative in your sexual relationship to make certain that your needs are met. It means assuming more responsibility for yourself. By doing so, you may lose some of the security of being taken care of, but, in turn, you gain a sense of autonomy that allows you to have sex if you want to or refuse if you're not in the mood. Some women get into the bind of resisting sex simply because their partner initiates it. They begin to feel that sex is something that is "done" to them, an activity in which they can make no choices. However, once you feel the freedom to initiate sex and take part in directing it, it can be as enjoyable for you as it is for your partner. Sherry used to freeze up when her husband made sexual advances toward her. But now she says, "I realize that I can be in control and do not have to be a spectator watching what he does to me. I stop and think for a moment, 'Do *I* want sex?' If the answer is no I tell him and if the answer is yes I can leap in and enjoy it." Laurie uses the vibrator during intercourse and really enjoys the fabulous feelings she didn't have before. She says, "Now I'm a willing partner and equal in initiating sex. Now I don't feel like pushing him away when he becomes amorous because I have the freedom to say 'No, I'm tired and let's try it tomorrow,' because now I'm being honest."

Frequently your sexual desire or lack of it will coincide with that of your partner, but even if it doesn't, masturbation provides each partner the freedom to express their individual sexual needs even when the other person is not in the mood to participate. Surprisingly enough, most couples' frequency of sexual contact rises rather than declines once the partners feel that they have the freedom to refuse sex if they choose to do so.

And that leads me to the last myth, the notion that sex "should" come naturally—that is, we should intuitively and automatically know what our partner likes and wants at a specific moment and our partner should be able to mind-read our desires. Perhaps the most important contribution to a satisfying sexual relationship is the ability to communicate what you like to your partner. Each of us is unique and the only way our partner can know what we want is if we tell him. We need to develop our own individual styles, and redefine sexuality so that it fits each of us individually. If we like one technique or position we can engage in it and if not, we can forget it, no matter what others say about it. The fact that we like or don't like a specific thing is reason enough for our doing or not doing it. And there is always the possibility that the activities we reject today may be acceptable tomorrow.

However, likes and dislikes often vary between sexual partners and compromises have to be made. For example, if your partner hates spinach and you really like it, there is no reason why you would have to give up spinach altogether. Either you'll prepare spinach less frequently or else you'll provide carrots for your partner and spinach for yourself. Likewise with sex. A couple can use certain positions occasionally, if they are enjoyable only for one person, while employing additional positions—some that are your favorites, some that are your partner's, and especially those that you both enjoy equally. If you both are getting what you want there is less likely to be resentment and conflict over sexual activities.

Actually, these myths may accurately describe some people's behaviors and needs at some time. However, the danger occurs when they harden into rules. You may find yourself intellectually thinking that some of these myths make little sense as rigid rules for behavior while emotionally continuing to respond in accordance with them. Changing basic beliefs takes time; they don't automatically vanish just because you confront them. Rather, positive personal experience is the most effective means of changing beliefs. For example, let's say that you had always been told, and therefore believed, that all frozen orange juice tasted the same, so you always bought the most inexpensive brand. Then you visited a friend for breakfast and the orange juice tasted fresh. When you inquired about it she told you that it was a different brand of frozen juice from the one you usually bought. You might then not only change brands of orange juice, but alter your belief that all frozen orange juice tastes alike. Similarly with sex; through personal experience, you can learn to identify your own needs, wants, and patterns of response. I am not issuing a blanket statement that sex in all forms is marvelous and that anything "should" go. Such a statement is as coercive as the religious doctrines that dictate that sex is only permissible for the purposes of procreation. To be sure, sex is fun, but each of us has a different idea of what "fun" means. Some of us may ride motorcycles for enjoyment while others play bridge, and there is plenty of room for these individual preferences. We have the right to choose what forms of sex are enjoyable for us. But let us look to our own common sense response and not the "shoulds" of others to make our decisions. Let us respect the rights and needs of others. While we explore our own needs and preferences, slowly and carefully, trying only the things that feel right to try at a particular time. In this way, we can escape the chains of myth and social stereotype and experience the freedom of expressing our authentic selves.

11: Partners

Once you are orgasmic through self-stimulation, the next step is sharing your sexuality—integrating the process into a sexual relationship with a partner. Whatever the nature of your partner relationship, you may have to confront some significant issues in order to make changes that will enable you to be orgasmic with a partner.

Before you even begin to talk to your partner about making changes in the sexual relationship, it is natural for you to wonder what response you'll get. Why should your partner want to make changes if he has found your former style of love-making enjoyable? If sex has not been satisfying for you and you've talked about it with your partner, your partner probably isn't totally satisfied either. If you've been faking orgasms and your partner is unaware of your dissatisfaction, there are still many benefits to making changes in your sexual routine—benefits for both of you.

Any couple's sex life can get into a rut after a period of time. Making alterations can sometimes provide a refreshing change. Just talking about sex and thinking about it at various times during the day can enhance your relationship.

Prolonging the love-making, making it a voluptuous meal rather than a quick snack can replace humdrum sex with real excitement. Spending the time enjoying the scenery along the way rather than doggedly focusing on the destination can result in a much more relaxing and sensuous experience. And the longer and more enjoyable the whole experience is, the more likely it is to include orgasm.

Self-stimulation has taught you about some things which arouse you. You now know some things that you can teach your partner which will add to the love-making experience. Teaching your partner what excites you sexually can result in relieving him of considerable performance pressure. Once he is comfortable with manual and other techniques, he will not need to maintain an erection for an extended period of time, or get an erection at all, to help you attain orgasm.

Sex, although only one aspect of a relationship, is an important aspect. Being close and communicating about sex can bring a deeper level of communication in all aspects of the relationship. Pleasing each other in bed can spread to pleasing each other in additional areas. Open sexual communication can mean the difference between sexual frustration and satisfaction.

The end results can be delightful—but getting to the end is not simple. As a matter of fact, the most difficult part often occurs in making the first move. How to bring up the subject of sex and how to discuss it openly presents great obstacles to many women. You may find yourself wanting to quit even before you've begun.

You may hesitate to talk to your partner for reasons that go deeper than a mere reluctance to talk openly about sex. You may be angry at your partner for many things that you haven't expressed openly. Some women feel powerless in their relationship. They may feel that the only time they can say no is in bed. If you say no or argue about what is really bothering you, you might fear that you will stir up a fight or even ultimately lose your partner. So maybe you take out your resentments by withholding sex. Some women acquiesce to sex, but get even with their partners by not having orgasms. We're all unfortunately too familiar with the martyred wife: "I'll go along with sex (or even initiate it), but I'll be so frustrated and miserable that you'll be sorry." Your partner may end up feeling lousy, but you will too. Meanwhile, your partner is unaware of what is *really* bothering you. For all too long, sex has been the battleground for other issues. If you're fighting on the wrong front, you can't possibly win. Maybe you could win, though, if you could argue about what *really* bothers you, leaving your sexual feelings for your partner uncontaminated by other, withheld, negative feelings.

Again, fears may get in the way. Deep down, you may fear that you really aren't sexual and that trying to change your orgasmic situation might only confirm this fear.

Some women find it difficult to ask for things for fear of being turned down. Jenny can't ask for anything until she is desperately in need. Then, if her request is refused, she feels devastated. She and other women like her, who have had no practice at making requests when the stakes are low, never learn to cope with the reactions that occur when they finally do make a request that is refused.

Also common is the fear of being engulfed if you let go and have an orgasm with your partner. You've learned to trust yourself and your own self-stimulation, but giving that power and control to a partner can be disquieting. You can't give up control unless you feel you have some. Therefore, gaining more control is a task that precedes learning to give it up. Control can be gained by telling your partner what you want. By practicing the Yes's and No's described in Chapter 4 you can be convinced that you can stop or say no any time you want to. Then, when you feel that you have more control over your sexual decisions, you may find that you feel secure enough to allow yourself to relax and let go.

Sherry was afraid to let her orgasmic feelings engulf her with her husband—even though she could enjoy those feelings when alone. She would find herself involuntarily holding back during partner love-making. With time and practice, however, she slowly learned to trust herself and her responses with her partner as well.

You may be afraid you'll hurt your partner's feelings and so you protect him by not doing anything about your lack of orgasmic response. You may be afraid of hurting his ego or threatening him. Is your partner really that fragile? Do you have to remain the pure little girl for him to feel like the potent man? If you become more responsive will he feel inferior as a man? There is no way to second-guess his reaction for sure, but you may be wasting years of sexual enjoyment for yourself while needlessly protecting him. It may be better to take a chance and attempt to make some changes. Keep in mind that making changes is not always easy, nor does it always happen without any unpleasant, guilty, or uncertain feelings. There is a risk involved, but generally far less of a risk than you might imagine.

The status quo might be unhappy, but at least you're familiar with it, and it feels safe. Rocking the boat and trying to make changes might produce a type of unhappiness for which you are unprepared. What happens if it fails? Then what? Or worse still, what happens if he stops loving you; or if he leaves you because of your attempts to change things? Granted, making changes in a relationship is difficult and potentially disruptive, but making no changes and remaining dissatisfied is usually far worse. Changes may not always be well received by your partner, he may not love them immediately. He may even be upset. But he can get over it—especially if you have a basically positive relationship. If you do take the risk and attempt to make the changes, you'll probably discover that your fears were exaggerated.

Negative male reactions to changing sexual behavior do occur, however, especially at the beginning. Many men are threatened by women masturbating and fear that they might be replaced by masturbation. Many men feel astounded that you would want to masturbate when they are there to meet your sexual needs. Initially masturbation may also be as unacceptable to him as it was to you. Remember your first reactions and maybe your inability to even say "masturbation" out loud. Both men and women have been brought up in the same culture and have been indoctrinated with similar feelings about self-stimulation.

It a man objects initially, he will probably mellow with time assuming that you care for him and that you're sincerely interested in making the sexual relationship better. You may want to let him know that many men react this way initially. It may help him to better understand and accept his response. Ann's husband felt better after she told him that the partners of other women in the group were threatened too.

Some men feel inadequate if you open the subject of sex—especially if they weren't previously aware that there was a problem. Until you explain the difficulty he may feel that your lack of orgasmic response is his fault. Even if your partner is aware that you have difficulty reaching orgasm, he may feel that his sexual technique is inadequate or that he is inadequate as a lover, especially if he accepts the myth that he "should" be the authority on sex rather than looking to you for more information and direction.

Both Angela's and Gloria's husbands were very threatened the first week of the group. Gloria's husband ejaculated prematurely several times and Angela's husband was unable to get an erection on two occasions. Within a week both problems had passed but Angela's husband threatened to divorce her if his problem were to continue and she refused to quit the group. It is interesting to note that Angela never threatened to divorce *him* if her problem continued.

Women are often willing to assume the role of patient, understanding, forgiving sexual companion. How ludicrous it would appear if roles were reversed and women usually had their orgasms first, rolled off their partners and went to sleep. If the man protested, the woman could explain that she was too tired to go on and apologize. I wonder how many men would acquiesce and say, "It's OK dear, it doesn't matter."

The group experiences indicate that most partners' reactions are positive and supportive, if not initially, then after a very short period of time. Some men are concerned that they won't be able to change enough to meet the needs of their partners. Harriet's husband was so desperately eager to please her that he was very worried about his ability to make the changes Harriet wanted.

Most men are very appreciative when they are finally given some information they can apply to love-making. These men have frequently tried everything they know and don't know what else to do to improve the situation. Getting assistance from a partner relieves them of the responsibility for finding a solution. Most men will cooperate once they understand how important the issue of your sex life is to you.

If you and your partner don't generally talk very openly about sex, bringing up the topic into general conversation can be tricky. Many couples are stuck in neutral silence: "I won't say anything if you won't and we'll both pretend there is no problem, that nothing is wrong." But ignoring a problem can insure that no solution will ever be found, especially if it hasn't worked itself out by now. Guard against playing "blackmail," that is when one person brings up a sensitive and touchy issue, the partner retaliates in kind. ("I won't bring up sex if you won't talk about my stock fiasco.") These pacts can destroy closeness and intimacy in a relationship and preclude deeper understanding and change. You want your partner to hear, but you don't want to make him angry, defensive, or hurt. It is difficult to insure that none of these negative reactions will occur. An initial negative reaction may be inevitable, but much of the reaction depends on the way you present the issue. You can use it as a sledge hammer—"You had better do this or else." Or, as a possibility for growth—"There are some things we could change that might make sex more enjoyable for both of us and improve our sex life." You can blame your partner—"It's all your fault that our sex life is so lousy, so *you* do something about it." Or, you can open up and share your feelings—"Our sex hasn't been the best it could be for me but if you would work on it with me I think there are some things we could do together that might make it better." Take the time to state your personal feelings and fears. Making accusations rarely brings about the desired results. You might want to explain that it is not his fault, but that you have also been unaware of how to change the situation; that now you have some ideas about how to change things; and you'd like his help.

Sarah had been faking orgasms but finally decided to approach the problem with her partner. She told him, "I'm having trouble reaching orgasm [to say the least—she'd never had an orgasm with a partner], but if you'll give me three hours of your time we can work on it." She gave him numerous directions during this time that they set aside; they stopped to rest for a while when things did not go well. But after stopping and taking the pressure off, Sarah got closer to having an orgasm than she ever had before, and these first three hours of experimentation remain a memorable experience for them both. Clearly, your initial approach can greatly influence the outcome.

Talking about sex when you have been faking orgasm presents a special difficulty. One woman warned the others not to tell their partners that they had been faking. She had faked for two years before marriage and two years after. Then, in the heat of an argument, she had told her partner the truth. As a result, their relationship had been going steadily downhill ever since. The negative response from her husband may very well have been a reaction to her using the confession of her faking as a weapon in the heat of an argument. In my experience, most women who have told their partners in a less emotionally charged atmosphere have not met with the same response. Nina was finally honest with her partner and to her surprise found that he was very willing to participate in couple counseling, even though before she had told him, she was sure he would never agree.

You might tell your partner that you are not sure you are having orgasms, or that you would like to make them better after reading this book. Carmen used to fake consistently. When she entered the group she told her partner she was going to a class in sexuality; she is now orgasmic but has never told him that she once wasn't. In general, follow your intuition and move only as quickly as you feel is prudent in your situation.

Even if your partner is a bit resistant or threatened at first, a loving attitude that takes his uneasiness into account can enable him slowly to feel more secure and more willing to participate. If your partner's initial response is negative, your tendency may be to just drop the subject and return to the status quo, even if it's unsatisfactory. However, persistence can bring positive results. Pam was orgasmic with masturbation but never with a partner. She decided that her sexuality was very important and that she wanted to spend time and energy working on it. She presented the idea to her partner who responded very negatively. He informed her that if she wanted to work on her sexuality she could do it elsewhere without his participation. Instead of giving up, Pam reiterated that it was important to her and suggested that perhaps he could agree to do just a few things. Finally, he reluctantly agreed to do the assignments. Pam moved slowly and didn't let his lack of enthusiasm get her down. Pam's partner fulfilled each assignment grudgingly, but nonetheless, their sex life really improved. They began having sex more frequently and both felt more sensual and excited than ever before. The night set aside for the homework was always a low point, but Pam made sure that the assignments were completed and, despite her partner's ill feelings about the program, their love-making improved.

Perhaps a good way for you to enlist your partner's co-operation would be to share this book with him. If he would read it too, he might better understand the framework for your ideas. In our groups the women are given some written material to read at home. Angela casually left the pamphlets lying around in hopes her husband would pick them up and read them. Unfortunately, he never took the hint or, if he did read the material, he never mentioned it. It might be a good idea to be more direct and let your partner know that you want him to have this information if that is the case.

Discussing sex can lead to closer, deeper feelings, even if it entails some disagreement. At the Medical Center in San Francisco, the Human Sexuality Program periodically presents a two-session sexuality education program. The first week is devoted to discussion of female sexuality and the second to male sexuality. When couples return the second week after completing the first session, they typically are enthusiastic because they have gone home and talked about sex in a way they never had before. Most of the women report that the sexual experience they had after the talk was one of the best they could remember. A few women have reported that a fight followed the discussion—in some cases a major fight—but that within a day or two they, too, had a close, warm, love-making session that would always stand out in their memories.

I can add only that talking about sex intimately, openly, and honestly results in improving a couple's ability to talk about other issues more directly. Sex is one of the most personal and difficult areas to discuss. However, once progress has been made in this area, it seems that more honest, open communication takes place in less emotionally charged areas as well.

If you can broach the topic of your sexual relationship with your partner, you have made the first very important step toward improving it. The first giant step counts for a lot, even if you have to take a small step backward later. Your partner may need some time to adjust to the idea of re-lating in a new way sexually. Men have fears, and can be up-tight about sex too. After all, they were socialized in the same society. For example, some men don't like to touch a woman's genitals; many feel it is morally wrong to stimulate the clitoris. Men may have hangups about nudity or may re-spond negatively toward a woman who is at all sexually as-sertive. Harriet's husband was extremely puritanical, but Harriet managed to make some changes in their sex life, by proceeding slowly.

Remember, if you do make some changes in yourself and your approach to sex, your partner will have to interact dif-ferently with you, because you will be different. Some women feel that their partners are hopeless and couldn't possibly change their attitudes toward sex. You may be amazed at the results when you try—not to change your partner's idea, but to change *your* role in the sexual relationship. He may not support you at first, but he may respond to the actual sexual experience positively. For change to occur, it is not necessary that your partner offer to make the changes or initiate them; what is necessary is that you attempt some changes and that he go along with your attempts.

I have given many words of warning and ways to prevent potential difficulties that might deter you from making the changes you desire. But many partners respond optimistically and favorably from the outset. Most lovers care enough about their partners to be willing to try almost anything that will increase their partner's happiness. Rather than being an obstacle, your partner could provide support and love enabling the two of you to transform the exploration of your orgasmic response into an enjoyable game.

Don't expect miraculous changes right away. Changes take time. Now is a time for experimentation. The next chapter contains some exercises you can work on with your partner. Allow yourself to relax and enjoy doing them. They have worked for many couples, and with the right approach, they may be helpful for you too.

12: Partner Exercises

As with the masturbation program, becoming orgasmic with a partner necessitates making the time to practice. Doing so is even more difficult when two people are involved, because now two people will have to make time and synchronize their schedules.

Most couples procrastinate and avoid spending the time to interact sexually, especially if their sex life has been less than satisfactory. But if you don't spend time together things most assuredly will not change. Remember the negative cycle that results from unsatisfying sex. The more negative experiences, the more both people will anticipate a negative experience even though they may try to keep their hopes up. This expectation in itself can create enough anxiety and resentment to preclude positive results. Fortunately, positive reinforcement can reverse this process. The more positive experiences you have, the more you will expect a positive experience, and you can relax, thereby facilitating positive results. Thus, positive experiences are extremely important from the very beginning. Making sure that the time set aside will be relaxing and fairly free from intrusions is absolutely necessary. Moving slowly, going only as far as feels comfortable, and making sure the experience is enjoyable are essential. Keeping communication open about reactions before, during and after is also critical to paving the way for successful and satisfying love-making.

As you begin to experiment, it might be helpful to try to reserve judgment about the exercises. Unless something really offends you or makes you uncomfortable, try it a few times. Then decide whether you like it and want to continue using it as one of your options, or if you want to discontinue it temporarily and possibly forever. Remember, all decisions apply only to the present—you can choose to disregard some exercise now, while remaining free to change your mind in the future. If something is making you uncomfortable, be sure to let your partner know. If you don't make yourself clear, your partner may interpret a negative response as a rejection of him rather than of the activity. Adding a positive "Maybe if you tried this" or "Doing it this way might be better," rather than a categorical "Stop" or "Don't do that," is far more instructive and more likely to receive a supportive response.

Since enjoyable sex entails much more than reaching orgasm, it's important to find out exactly what you *are* feeling during sex with a partner, so that you can begin to isolate problem areas. The best way to do this is to forget totally about orgasms for the moment. Pretend this is another fact-finding mission and your only assignment is to relax and enjoy the scenery. Concentrate on the sensual feelings. We sometimes put so much emphasis on the goal, orgasm, that we lose track of what we are actually feeling during the sensual experience. Dr. Harvey Caplan, a colleague of mine, tells a story that illustrates the point beautifully. When he was sixteen and just beginning to date and drive, he couldn't wait to park and neck with his current girlfriend. When they stopped driving and began kissing his mind wasn't on the kissing but on how he could touch her breast. Finally, when he succeeded in that conquest, he couldn't enjoy the feel of her breast because he was already concerned with how he could unfasten her bra. And so on and on. He was so busy thinking ahead that he could not fully appreciate the feelings of the moment. Many of us still find ourselves in that position today—so concerned about the future, or what's going to happen next that we don't appreciate the present.

The first partner exercise is simply to concentrate on what's happening in the present when you make love. *Do not* allow yourself to have an orgasm. Instead, see what the contact of your partner's skin against your own feels like. Soak up the pleasure like a sponge. Actively keep your mind tuned to the present. See what happens when you just relax and enjoy the sensations. Peggy had been separated for eight months from her husband, with whom she had been orgasmic. Although she had slept with a number of other men since the separation she had been unable to reach orgasm with any of them. She thought it might be guilt over leaving her husband or some other emotion that she wasn't aware of; she simply couldn't figure out the situation. When she entered the group she was involved with a lover whom she had known before she met her husband. She felt comfortable with him and had even been orgasmic with him some ten years earlier. Now she was at a total loss as to what to do to overcome the block. In the first session we instructed the women to attend to the sensations of the moment and forget about orgasm. For the first time in eight months Peggy had an orgasm with a partner, and continued to experience orgasm regularly thereafter. It appears that all she needed was permission to relax and enjoy sex for enjoyment's sake; then, following the natural process, orgasm occurred.

Find a two-week stretch when you will be able to set aside an hour each day to do the exercises 2-10. In their therapy, Masters and Johnson advocate a ban on intercourse during the time it takes to complete the initial few partner exploration assignments. I also encourage a ban on orgasms, even through masturbation. During the days it takes to accomplish the first few partner exercises, try to forget that both intercourse and orgasm exist. Discuss the no orgasm/no intercourse ban with your partner. The ban should last for less than one week if you do the exercises daily. Deciding not to have intercourse or orgasm can help relieve the anxiety and concern that surrounds sex in which intercourse is the defined goal. Also, preventing orgasmic release while concurrently participating in erotic and sensual activities will help keep you in a sexual mood and maintain a high level of sexual arousal, even though it may prove to be a bit frustrating.

Although your partner cannot have intercourse with you, there is no reason why he cannot have orgasms. The procedure is not designed as punishment for a supportive lover. You can bring your partner to orgasm orally or manually, or your partner can stimulate himself to orgasm after an exercise is completed. The two of you can decide ahead of time how you want to work this out. Gloria and her husband decided that if he wanted her to manually stimulate him to orgasm after they had completed an assignment, she would do so. Whereas Betty and her husband agreed that they both could benefit from the exercises; he was willing to share the ground rules that she was going to abide by—no intercourse and no orgasm until a later exercise.

Couples sometimes break this no intercourse/no orgasm rule soon after they begin working on the exercises. Some women complained that their partner insisted on intercourse and they felt that they had to acquiesce, or that they initiated sex because they felt guilty. Since intercourse, at this early stage, rarely results in orgasm, the woman is frequently left feeling angry and resentful toward her partner for not really caring about her needs. But remember that the woman agreed to participate. She could have refused and her partner could have achieved release in another manner. Other women break the rule because they feel so aroused that they are sure they'll have an orgasm if they have intercourse this time. They usually don't and then are doubly disappointed. One or two experiences of feeling aroused is usually not sufficient to reverse past negative experiences. As soon as intercourse begins, the old worries and concerns generally come flooding back.

If you do break the rule and negative results occur, don't be concerned, just backtrack and begin over again, hopefully with greater resolve to follow the instructions more carefully.

Touching is usually very important to women, often more important in terms of total responsivity than for most men. However, being attuned to the dimension of touch can greatly enhance a man's sexual experience too. Many women's biggest complaint is that their partners do not spend enough time touching their bodies and genitals before intercourse begins. Lydia and Ellen both resented being awakened in the middle of the night for love-making because their partners would start directly with intercourse, with no preliminary touching. Ellen claimed that having her mother rub salve on her chest when she had a cold was more sensual than having sex with her husband. Confining your activity to touching may seem like a regression when you're concerned about orgasm, but it really isn't. It is a way to get back to the initial building blocks of sexual excitement, a new way to approach sexual contact; a way to revisit adolescence when just touching and kissing could send one's body into a frenzy.

Spend the hour on the first two days revisiting the experience of touching by giving each other an information massage. This is Partner Exercise 2. All too many couples who have difficulties with their sexual relationship avoid any touching of one another—even nonsexual touching (touching whose primary goal is to produce pleasure, but not necessarily arousal) because of the expectation that touching has to lead to sex. This in itself can create a physical distance between the two people. Consequently, the return to touching can provide an initial bridge in re-establishing feelings of closeness. Nonsexual touching can be a very enjoyable and sensuous experience and an important part of a relationship.

Begin with an area that is far from the center of your body: hands, feet, head, or face. Pick as the one area to be massaged the one that would be most pleasurable for you. For example, if you have very ticklish feet, a foot massage would probably not be a good choice. Your partner should pick one of the areas also, but it need not be the same choice as yours. Decide who will give the first half-hour massage. You could do this by mutual decision or by flipping a coin. The point of the exercise is for the person who is doing the massaging to explore for the sake of whatever satisfaction is in it for her or him, *not to please the partner*. Don't worry about your technique—this is just for you. The exercise is designed so that the giver will relearn to appreciate the pleasures touching can have, in and of itself.

If your partner has chosen to receive a hand massage, pick up the hand gently and carefully. Caringly explore it in detail. Investigate nails, fingers, palm; lightly follow the vein structure and all the tiny lines on the skin. Keep as much of your skin in contact with your partner's as possible. Use the fronts and backs of your hands to maintain physical contact. Explore the softer and rougher skin textures. Apply some oil and massage more deeply, becoming familiar with the joints and the deeper muscles and bones. Remember, the person massaging is doing it for his or her own satisfaction, and to increase his or her own knowledge.

The person receiving the massage need only relax and enjoy it. This person has one responsibility and that is to tell the person giving the massage to discontinue doing something if it is painful or uncomfortable. You can make any pleasurable noises you might want to make, but during this exercise don't ask for anything unless it is to tell your partner that the massage is becoming uncomfortable. If the person receiving the massage becomes uncomfortable about being touched, cut down the time spent. Do it for no longer than one-half hour this first time.

After one person has finished giving the massage, switch places, making the receiver the giver. Angela's husband enjoyed giving his wife a massage, but he was uncomfortable about accepting one. He was very work oriented and found considerable difficulty in allowing himself to experience pleasure. In this case, they began with his receiving only a two-minute massage and built the time up slowly as he gradually learned to become a little more comfortable with receiving pleasure. In our culture, where the puritan work ethic is so strong, many of us feel guilty and lazy when we spend time giving and receiving pleasure. We are programmed always to have a purpose, to strive, to succeed, but not to relax and enjoy just being alive and feeling good.

Complete this exercise on at least two successive days (picking a different area to be massaged the second day) before moving on. After each massage session, sit down together for ten minutes and discuss what it was like to give and receive the massage. If you are finding the exercise particularly difficult to do, or if it is very uncomfortable for one or both of you, cut down the amount of time you spend on the massaging and extend the number of days, building up the time slowly until you can massage for one-half hour with a fair degree of comfort. This is not a sexual exercise. It is designed to orient you toward touching for the pleasure of touching. *The Massage Book* by George Downing is a good reference if you desire to explore, in further depth, massage as an activity.

Partner Exercise 3 is designed to go a little further. The touching will be aimed at awakening the whole body to sensations of touch. It will also provide an experience in which each of you has the opportunity to be alternately active and passive in a sexual situation. Furthermore, it will encourage open and direct communication about sensual stimulation.

This exercise is similar to the sensate focus advocated by Masters and Johnson.[1] Again, set aside an hour and decide who will go first. By this time you may have decided to take turns on succeeding days. Make sure the room is warm enough for you to be comfortable in the nude. Create a sensual atmosphere and setting. A sensual, but not too filling meal may provide an enticing prelude.

The exercise is aimed at a total sensual body experience. Gather as many props as you can find—feathers, flannel, wool, velvet, satin, brushes, oils, powder. Explore your lover's body everywhere except for the genitals and the breasts. Often, the exploration of these two areas lead to the expectation of intercourse and may cause some women to feel tense or wary thus preventing them from enjoying this exercise fully.

The purpose of this exercise is not to arouse, but to explore. Again, the person doing the exploring or the giving should do so for his or her own satisfaction primarily and for the partner's satisfaction only secondarily. The more the giver is enjoying the giving, the more the one who is the receiver is likely to enjoy the experience.

The person on the receiving end should relax and savor being the receiver. To enjoy sex more, there is value to learning to be temporarily selfish; to allow yourself to enjoy sensual pleasure with no other obligation. The additional requirement for this exercise, however, is for the receiver to let the giver know how things are going. The receiver can make some requests, "A little higher; harder; that tickles" etc. Noises indicating pleasure are valuable; nonverbal communication is very important. By placing your hand over your partner's you can help guide him to a specific area, pressure, or type of stroking you desire. Experiment with all these methods of communication. The giver can also ask questions. Always be honest about what you want to do; never offer anything if you don't really want to do it. Again, the getter is responsible for letting the giver know whenever a certain touch is either irritating or not pleasurable. It is important that the giver not do anything he or she doesn't want to do. In real life, requests are often refused, so you need not feel obligated just because someone asks something of you. You are just as free to say yes or no as the person making the request.

After a half hour, switch places. You get no extra points for giving longer than the assigned half hour, and your partner is not required to give more just because you did. Sticking to the time that you agreed on helps eliminate the resentment that one person may feel about giving more than his or her share and the indebtedness that the other person may feel. Again, if one-half hour apiece is too long, shorten the exercise time and build up slowly.

Maintaining the communication is essential, so after each exercise is over, discuss how each of you felt during the sensual body experience. What was it like to be assertive? Passive? What was it like to experience your partner as assertive and passive? Are there any other things left unsaid? Any things that may not even be related to the exercises? This is your time to communicate openly. Remember, still no intercourse and no orgasm for the woman.

Exercise 4 is called the sexological exercise. This exercise enables each of you to teach the other about your unique genital responses. Again, decide who will take the first turn. One of you will explore the other's genitals first visually and then by touching. If your genitals are being explored, your partner should explore them in the same manner you explored them by yourself as described in Chapter 5. Your partner should locate all the parts, touch the various organs and areas to see which are most sensitive to touch. If the inner lips are held between the thumb and forefinger of each hand, a gentle tug will show the effect of the clitoris and clitoral hood which approximates the amount of clitoral stimulation that commonly occurs during intercourse. A finger could be inserted in the vagina, up to the end of the first joint of the index finger. Then the finger could be crooked slightly. If the vaginal opening is thought of in terms of a clock face, the part of the vagina closest to the abdomen, while the woman is lying down, would be twelve o'clock; firm, gentle pressure could be exerted on each "hour" of the clock. Are any of these points especially sensitive, pleasurable? If so, let him know. Contract the PC muscle when the finger is still inserted. Can he feel the pressure? Let your partner know how each part responds to touch and what kinds of touch feel best. A lubricant or oil should be used if the touching is experienced as irritating.

When it is the partner's turn to be explored the illustrations in Masters and Johnson's *Human Sexual Response* could be used as a guide. His genitals could be examined visually using sufficient light; the presence or absence of an erection makes no difference as far as carrying out the exam goes, but an erection might change your partner's perception of the touching, since some areas of the penis might be more sensitive when it is erect. Which areas are most pleasurable when touched? The right side? The left? The midline on the bottom side? The head? Which is preferred, a light movement of the fingers over the shaft or a more solid stroking that massages the structures below the skin? How hard can you squeeze the shaft near the glans without it hurting? Watch the muscles of the scrotum (the sack that holds the testicles) move when you stroke the inner thigh.

After you've explored each other's genitals, talk about what it was like to be explored and to explore. What did each of you like? Dislike? What did you learn from the experience?

Probably at least four days of abstinence have now passed and you may feel fairly aroused. The next exercise, the fifth, may not be a very easy one, but it can be important. It's time now to bring in everything you have learned about your own body and share it with your partner by stimulating yourself in the presence of your partner.

Many people respond to this assignment with horror. "I couldn't do *that!*" "My partner would be disgusted," "I would be so embarrassed." However, Rosenberg claims that "a couple that can learn to masturbate each other effectively with just the right timing for pleasure can accomplish a more creative and satisfying sexual union."[2] Since each of you has a unique way in which you like to be touched to reach orgasm, showing your partner how you stimulate yourself can be helpful in teaching him how to stimulate you more pleasurably. Merely describing what you like may not be quite sufficient. Try to ignore any negative feelings and push beyond. At least broach the subject to your partner as a way to begin.

When I realized that we would have to assign this exercise to the women in the groups, at first I told myself it wasn't necessary—we could skip this exercise in the progression. But I knew it was important that a woman be able to go and have an orgasm in the presence of her partner and this could be an easy way to achieve this. So many women are afraid they'll look ugly or that their partner won't like it, and these thoughs can inhibit expression of sexual feelings when a partner is present.

In the groups we discovered that doing this exercise is not necessarily difficult, some couples don't experience any shyness or discomfort at all. Others had to prepare themselves mentally for days before they could complete this exercise.

Because this may be a difficult assignment, I cannot emphasize enough how important it is to talk about it thoroughly before you begin. Talk about your discomfort. Just because you're not totally comfortable doesn't mean you have to discard the exercise. It is important for both you and your partner to discuss feelings about this exercise. Together decide on the best way to carry out the exercise if you choose to do it, so the two of you will be as comfortable as possible. You might prefer to masturbate side by side. Or, your partner can hold you while you masturbate or your partner can just watch if you find being touched a distraction. If it is really difficult, you might try having your partner turn away and not look at you the first time and then try again the next day with your partner watching.

Don't be surprised if you don't reach orgasm the first or

second time you try it. Many women need to do the exercise a few times before they feel comfortable enough in the situation to let go.

The next exercise, Exercise 6, is designed to further open communication on sexual touching and to teach you to direct your partner in the type of touch that is most stimulating for you. Of course, there is no *one* kind of pressure or stroking that will be enjoyable at all times. The kind of touch that is stimulating will change with your level of excitement; this exercise helps you to practice keeping the communication lines open throughout the love-making experience.

Decide who will be first. That person should lie on the bed on his/her back while the other person sits or lies beside. Once you are in position, have the person doing the touching run both of his or her hands over the body of the other person. The partner being explored should have his or her hands resting lightly over the explorer's hands. Betty found that she liked her partner to spread his fingers apart and then when she placed her hand over his, she could fit her fingers between his and thus guide his hands and touch her own body at the same time. The explorer can explore everywhere, genitals included, but it's probably best to begin with other body areas first. Feel the skin textures, muscles, bones, and hair. Touch lightly with an almost feathery touch, then more firmly, try circular stroking, figure eights, using the tips of your fingers and your whole hand. Explore your partner's erogenous areas: inner thighs, breasts and nipples, genitals, and the special areas uniquely sensitive to that individual such as ears, back of neck, stomach, feet, etc.

The person being explored should practice giving explicit reactions, both verbal and nonverbal, to the exploring partner. Let your partner know what feels good, where and how, in a way that is comfortable for you. Suggest some areas and types of touching you think you might enjoy. Don't settle for saying, "Everything you do feels good," but begin to state your preferences honestly. When your partner moves on to stimulating your genitals, use your own hands to guide your partner's both to the area you would like explored and the pressure and kind of stroking you prefer. When you switch roles to that of the exploring partner, try to use the information you learned from watching your lover's self-stimulation on the previous day. Can you duplicate that stimulation with assistance from your partner?

The object of the exercise is to enjoy the stimulation and communicate your likes and dislikes to your partner. But if you feel very aroused, somehow let your partner know and explore further with the kinds of touching that might lead to orgasm. You may want to join your partner in exploring your own body by giving yourself the kind of stimulation that can bring you to orgasm. A sexual relationship can be so much more rewarding if there are no rules and regulations restricting touching. Many couples subscribe to the rule: I touch only your genitals and you touch only mine. However, when both people can touch the partner and themselves as well, sexual enjoyment can be doubled. Nobody "gives" anybody else an orgasm—it's a mutual process. The heads and bodies of both partners are closely involved.

The next exercise, Exercise 7, consists of transforming what has always been condescendingly labeled "foreplay" into a sexual experience that is important in itself. The ban on intercourse remains during this exercise. I know that this will mean a five-day abstinence up to this point but bear with it for just one more day. Tomorrow the exercise will include intercourse, but today it is essential to omit it.

Intercourse has always been considered "real sex" while "foreplay" has been a preliminary—something done primarily for the woman's pleasure. The touching, the manual and oral stimulation that precedes intercourse is extremely pleasurable for most women, but in the groups we found it seemed to be equally enjoyable for men once they ceased to see it as a chore they had to dutifully perform for a partner's benefit. Once men are relieved of some of the performance pressure that has historically been heaped upon them, they, too, can be passive, relax, and enjoy having their entire body stimulated by a partner.

Set aside an hour to elaborate on all the kinds of stimulation that precede and follow intercourse. While you and your partner are lying together, each of you take turns being aggressive and passive; also stimulate each other simultaneously. Be as creative as you'd like to be. Possibly enact some of the fantasies you may have had or elaborate on all the kinds of caressing you enjoy. An hour is a fairly long time, so relax and move slowly. Enjoy the process—make the process the goal. Keep communicating and keep each other informed about what feels good.

Again, orgasm is not the goal. If it happens, that's fine, but don't strive for it. Eventually orgasm will occur—usually after you have introduced changes in the love-making that make the experience a more exciting one for you. You may have to retrain yourself to detect and respond to sensual pleasure before stimulation can build to the level of orgasm.

Learning to appreciate and respond to sexual pleasure is analogous to learning to appreciate and respond to a piece of music. The first time you listen to a certain piano concerto, you may respond at one level. With future listening experiences, melodies, contrasts, and various nuances that were not apparent the first time become apparent. Then you can begin to respond to the piece at a different level. Of course, if while you're listening to the music, you're also attending to the traffic noise outside, thinking about the grocery bill, or wondering how the piece will end, you won't be able to enjoy the experience as it is unfolding. The same holds true for sexual appreciation. Appreciating and responding to sexual stimulation requires devoting more time to sexual interaction, becoming more comfortable communicating to your partner about the kind of touch you like, and focusing on the touch and pleasure as opposed to the orgasm. Consequently, it may be necessary to practice each exercise a number of times as part of your usual sexual experience with your partner before orgasm results.

The next exercise, Exercise 8, includes everything that has taken place before, plus intercourse. By this time each of you should have learned a great deal about the kind of stimulation that the other prefers. During this exercise, the communication lines should remain open as usual. Remember that you have a full hour to devote to the love-making so there is no need to rush right into intercourse.

When you are highly aroused and feel you are ready to begin having intercourse, let your partner know and get into the female astride position. In the female astride position, the man lies stretched out on his back between the legs of the woman who kneels over him, vagina directly above the penis. Her face can be facing his head or feet. The woman can then insert the penis. Assuming this position may feel like an interruption in the flow of love-making and may lower the woman's level of sexual excitation for a while, but it is not a cause for concern. Once effective stimulation is begun again, the level of excitement will generally rise.

For this part of the exercise, it is important that the man

remain relatively inactive. It is up to the woman to control the speed and manner of thrusting by moving her pelvis up and down, back and forth, or in a circular motion, a movement some women find particularly stimulating. At the same time, she should consistently and continuously stimulate the clitoral area with her fingers or with a vibrator. She should assume total control of the sex act. Don't expect to have an orgasm, just enjoy the pleasure of having the vagina and clitoral areas stimulated at the same time.

Most women automatically make two assumptions. The first is that the partner is not enjoying it. The best way to be sure about this is to ask. Samantha was constantly asking her partner if he was enjoying pleasing her and was amazed to find that he was. Finally she realized that her assumption that he wasn't enjoying it was an excuse for her to feel as if she didn't deserve all the attention and pleasure. It's good to keep in mind that your partner probably enjoys giving pleasure as much as you enjoy giving your partner pleasure.

Your partner may be concerned that he will have an orgasm before you do and may try to hold back. If he is feeling an orgasm approaching, he need not hold back, but should just relax and concentrate on the sensations. He can focus all his energy into the sensations he feels in his penis and if an orgasm approaches, let it take over. If this happens there is no reason for the woman to stop and consider the exercise over. In many cases the man is capable of maintaining a partial or even full erection if the pelvic movement is continued, but even if the erection is totally lost, the woman can continue to move slowly—not enough to cause the penis to come out, but enough to enjoy feeling it while continuing the stimulation in the clitoral area. An orgasm can still be experienced with your partner inside, even if his penis is not erect. If the man has an orgasm first, it can be a very positive experience for some women since they can then relax and enjoy their own stimulation once their feeling of responsibility for the partner's pleasure is eliminated.

The second and more pervasive assumption is the woman's belief that it is taking her too long to climax—a common concern of women who experience difficulty reaching orgasm. And, ironically, as soon as they begin worrying about how long it is taking, it begins to take even longer. Louise used to blame her husband for the short duration of their love-making. But then she realized that it was her own fear that the feelings wouldn't come, that was causing her to hurry the experience. Beth would get to the level where she felt aroused and then would feel she had had her quota of time and would turn her attention back to her husband. Both women used worrying about time as a way to terminate their own pleasure and cut off orgasm.

A woman's orgasm does take time and when a woman is first learning, it may take even longer. Gebhard found that among couples who regularly spend twenty-one minutes or longer on foreplay, only 7.7 per cent of the women failed to reach orgasm.[3] Relaxed and lengthy lovemaking can greatly enhance the woman's sexual experience. So before you even begin making love, set aside sufficient time. Place a clock where you can see it easily; you'll be amazed at how slowly an hour of love-making passes. Continue the stimulation in an uninterrupted manner for as long as is necessary for orgasm to occur. If you feel frustrated at some point, relax and just hold each other, or do whatever relaxes you until the frustration subsides. Remember, just as having an orgasm the first time through self-stimulation took time, having it with a partner takes a while too. It took Sarah one and a quarter hours the first time. The time does get shorter with practice, as the feelings become more familiar. If this exercise doesn't work the first time, don't be concerned. Repeat it over the next few days with whatever variations you prefer. You may have to practice this technique a number of times before you are successful. There is no rush. The only crucial part is that the woman continuously stimulate herself, while the man's penis is inserted. There are other positions that can be devised that afford access to the clitoral area during intercourse. These include: 1) the woman kneeling and the man, also kneeling, and entering the vagina from the rear; 2) the lateral position in which the man lies on his side with the woman lying parallel to him, her back against his front and his bottom leg between her legs; 3) an "X"-shaped position in which the man lies on his side, and the woman sits perpendicular to him, with her legs flexed over his side with the penis and vagina in proximity.

Once orgasm with the partner's penis inserted is achieved, the woman may still be interested in helping her lover learn to stimulate her manually to orgasm. She may want her partner to be more active and he may want to be more involved too.

The next exercise, Exercise 9, involves teaching your partner to stimulate the clitoral area manually. This requires a gradual aproach for two reasons. First, your partner cannot know instantly the feelings you have, as you know them when you stimulate yourself, and so he may not be immediately aware of what you want at a particular moment. It is up to you to communicate this as the love-making proceeds. Second, it takes some time to get used to the type of stimulation your lover provides because it will be as individual to that person as your likes and dislikes are to you. Try to have your partner adjust his technique to become more compatible with your preferences, and also try to accommodate your responses to the stimulation afforded by your partner.

In this exercise, decide how much time you want your partner to spend stimulating you. It might be as short as two minutes the first time, or as long as an hour. Set aside a comfortable time period. The amount of time can be gradually increased with each succeeding practice session. Then guide your partner by putting your hands over his. Your lover will have seen how you stimulate yourself and will already have a basic idea of how to touch you, but you may have to supply the specifics. What feels good may change as your level of excitation changes.

Sarah asked her boyfriend Joe if he would devote three hours to stimulating her because that was how long she thought it would take for her to reach orgasm. She tried Kegeling while he stimulated her, and various fantasies. Finally she began concentrating on the pleasure she was feeling and then pretended that the feelings were those of orgasm. No sooner did she pretend orgasm was occurring than one actually did. Joe felt great about it and said, "It only took one and a quarter hours. We have lots of time left, let's do it again."

The last exercise, Exercise 10, consists of your partner's applying clitoral stimulation during intercourse. This exercise is last because it may be more difficult to be orgasmic when your partner is controlling the stimulation. It is not last because it is best; the only measure of what is best is the amount of satisfaction derived from a sexual experience. The positions described for Exercise 9 are applicable to this exercise. The only prerequisite for a particular position is that the woman's clitoral area be available for manual stimulation. The male partner should apply the stimulation in an uninterrupted manner and with an intensity which the woman finds arousing.

I have consciously left out exercises which focus on orgasm without direct clitoral stimulation. After you have progressed this far, you may choose to stop direct clitoral stimulation short of orgasm if the penile thrusting provides sufficient stimulation.

After Exercise 5, when orgasm is allowed again, it is important to continue the masturbation exercises between partner sessions. Being sexually responsive requires both technique and practice. As indicated in Chapter 9, the closer the masturbation positions and activities approximate those employed during love-making, the easier it will be to experience orgasm with a partner.

Remember, learning these procedures takes time. The majority of women in the groups required three to eight months of practicing the exercises—which they integrated into their usual love-making—before they were comfortably orgasmic with a lover.

The exercises in this chapter have been directed toward restructuring your sexual relationship to meet needs expressed by many women. Most women find it enjoyable to have an orgasm at some time during love-making, but when or how the orgasm is achieved is not important. Even having an orgasm at all is sometimes unimportant. You may enjoy making love to your partner and feel no need to experience orgasm. You may feel tired or preoccupied with other concerns and just being sexually close may be a comfort.

Some women need to spend time in a relationship and get to know a partner fairly well before feeling free to express sexual preferences and sexual feelings. A number of women in the groups changed their attitudes toward partners and love-making as a result of the group learning experience. Cindy lost interest in casual affairs and now feels strongly that the man she is interested in should be a considerate lover; she is interested in quality rather than quantity now.

Changing your orgasmic responsivity with a partner takes not only time but also motivation. If either is lacking, and a haphazard approach to the process results, chances for success are lessened. Basic attitudes about sexuality change only over time and with the positive reinforcement of satisfying sexual experiences. The more successful sexual encounters you have, the more likely you are to expect a satisfying experience and hence have it materialize. Caring, loving, being intimate and sexual all require effort, sensitivity to the other person, and honest communication. It is both as easy and as difficult as that.

13: Sexual Expansion

Expansion and innovation in your sexual relationship could result in a heightening of sexual interest and pleasure, whether or not the various options always lead to orgasm. Depending upon the individual, expansion can occur in many directions: innovative coital techniques, innovative non-coital techniques, increased frequency of sex, integration of sexual paraphernalia, new sexual partners, same sex partners, group sex, etc. Sexual relationships can expand and grow in breadth and in depth. The important thing is to begin to express your sexuality more freely within the confines of the sexual boundaries with which you feel comfortable—to be able to explore further while still observing whatever moral, religious, intuitive, or common-sense feelings you have about sex.

An easy way to begin sexual expansion is to try a one-time experiment with something new and different for the sheer pleasure of just seeing what it is like. The innovation need not be monumental. An interesting touch, no matter how small, can enhance sexual interaction. Nina experimented by initiating a shower with her husband; both soaped and washed each other in a sensuous way. This was the first time she had ever initiated anything having to do with sex. She was pleased with the results and her husband was delighted. Sherry changed the furniture in the bedroom around to create a more sensual setting. Evelyn and her husband spent one night in a motel to feel really free from their children; she could then experiment with making as much noise during love-making as she wanted. Male and female stripteases, sensuous meals by candlelight, thorough body massages, or even parking and necking on a high hill with a view can provide new sensual experiences.

Or, try changing roles. One night one partner could take complete charge; the other partner could do so the next time. Do you have any fears about being the initiator? If so, discuss them with your partner ahead of time. Just bringing the fears into the open can make them less ominous.

Fantasies could be shared before, after, or during lovemaking. Explicit sexual conversation can be very arousing for some people. Cindy told the group that she really enjoyed using four-letter words during sex.

Despite old laws remaining on the books that define oral sex as a perversion punishable by a prison term, the Playboy Foundation Study found that more than 80 per cent of single males and females under thirty-five and about 90 per cent of married persons under twenty-five had practiced cunnilingus (the term for oral contact with the female genitals) and/or fellatio (the equivalent term for oral contact with the penis) in the year of the survey.[1] Obviously very few of the people interviewed are concerned about the legality of the practice; today it is very rare for anyone to be arrested and punished for participating in oral sex. Clearly, if so many people find oral sex enjoyable and sexually satisfying, and since there is no evidence that it is harmful, it should not be considered a crime. In many states it is in fact no longer considered illegal, but sexual mores change very slowly.

David Reuben makes the following incorrect statements: "The most presumably undersexed man or woman will be brought to an explosive orgasm by using this technique providing they are willing to do so";[2] "One of the best methods of assuring orgasm in the so-called frigid woman and encouraging a strong erection in a questionably potent man is this powerful form of total sexual stimulation."[3] Reuben makes oral sex sound like the sexual panacea, which it certainly is not; preference for these activities, as with other forms of sexual stimulation, vary with the individual. However, many women find cunnilingus highly stimulating for a number of reasons. First of all, as with manual stimulation, the mouth and tongue provide direct clitoral stimulation, but this stimulation is much softer and gentler than that provided manually; also, saliva acts as a natural lubricant. In addition, oral sex leaves the hands free to stimulate other sexually responsive areas such as the breasts and thighs.

Nevertheless, many women experience negative feelings about oral sex which often stem from negative feelings they have about their genitals. Women who consider their genitals "dirty" may expect their partner to find oral contact with the genitals unpleasant. Because of this expectation, they cannot allow themselves to relax and enjoy the stimulation; instead, they protect a partner from this "distasteful" experience by preventing the partner from orally stimulating the genitals. But the woman doesn't have to protect her partner, she can ask her partner whether or not he finds oral contact with her genitals pleasant. Some men, as well as some women, may indeed be uncomfortable with oral sex and may need a period of time working at a slow pace to adjust to this activity; others may not want to undertake it at all.

Jane had to overcome the feeling that oral sex was degrading to the person doing it. She always stopped her husband when he engaged in oral sex because she felt that performing it put him in an unmanly position. Debbie, who was in a lesbian relationship, hesitated to participate in oral sex for fear that she would not be good at it. After seeing *Behind the Green Door,* a pornographic film, Debbie and her lover talked about oral sex. Somehow, after discussing it and seeing the movie, Debbie became comfortable with the idea.

Some women may find it unpleasant for a partner to ejaculate in their mouth, while others enjoy the sensations. If this experience is uncomfortable for you, but you enjoy fellatio, work out a signal with your partner so that he can warn you just before ejaculation will occur. Some couples find that a man's tap on the woman's head at the appropriate moment can solve this problem.

When you first begin to explore oral sex, it is advisable to do so slowly. Talk about it with your partner; share your feelings together before you begin. Take a bath or shower together as a prelude to the experience. In this way, you may feel more secure about the cleanliness of your genitals and those of your partner. Decide ahead of time that if either of you becomes uncomfortable, that person will communicate the discomfort to the partner and both will stop and return to more familiar love-making techniques. Make sure that you are in a comfortable position. Begin by kissing the stomach area, the thigh area. For the first time, just brushing the mouth rapidly across a partner's genitals may be best. Expand the time slowly. Kathy Kelly, in her unpublished *Radical Sex Manual,* suggests, "Build-up is important. Slightly increase the pressure and the speed of stimulation . . ."[4] Probably the most important thing is to maintain a steady uninterrupted rhythm of stimulation once an intensity and a pressure which is arousing to the woman has been reached.

Oral sex may not prove the panacea to sexual problems, as Reuben suggests, but it can be an enjoyable addition to a sexual relationship.

A variety of coital positions can enhance one's sex life. The important thing is to find positions that are not painful or uncomfortable for either partner. A position favored by one partner may not be the favorite of the other, but couples are free to employ several different intercourse positions during one session of love-making. Some positions may be better if the woman wants to stimulate herself and others if the partner applies the stimulation.

Variations in coital positions are more widely employed today than in years past. The recent Playboy Foundation Study shows that the woman on top position is used at least occasionally by nearly 75 per cent of all married couples in 1972; only 30 per cent used this position in the 1930–40s. Also, statistics show that four times as many married couples today use the rear entry position as was true in Kinsey's study. Twice as many use the side by side position, and almost three times as many use the sitting position at least occasionally.[5]

The anal area can be highly erogenous; many women enjoy oral as well as manual stimulation of the anus. Anal intercourse can be enjoyable although it is not very widely practiced among heterosexual couples. The Playboy Foundation Study states that "about a quarter of married couples under thirty-five use anal intercourse at least now and then."[6]

The anal sphincter muscle is a strong muscle and may not be penetrated easily at first. The "missionary" position in which the woman is on her back with her knees or legs raised making the anus accessible to the penis may be a good position to begin with. A lubricant jelly (not Vaseline) can facilitate the process, as can a lubricated condom. The latter both lubricates the anal entrance and protects the male's urethra against infection by any bacteria that may be present in the rectum.

Once in this position the penis can be inserted slowly and in a way that is comfortable. Many women prefer the male to be passive at the beginning so that the woman can control both the rate of insertion and the thrusting movements. Later, the woman may be comfortable with her partner taking a more active role. Hygienically, it is important that the male not insert his penis or fingers in the vagina after anal intercourse or anal play without washing thoroughly, because certain bacteria in the rectum when spread to the vagina can cause vaginal infections.

There are a number of sexual life styles that this book has not dealt with explicitly, but I hope it has been implied in the philosophy of the book; premarital sex, extramarital sex, group sex, homosexuality, bisexuality, and abstinence are all options. An acceptance of individuality can enable each person to express her own needs without it being seen as a threat to the individuality of another. It entails acceptance of one's own life style without trying to forcibly impose one's desires on others. The ability to say yes or no to things because a person wants to or doesn't want to participate, and not because some leaders of the society say it is right or wrong, can lead to a peaceful coexistence in which people may really be able to learn from one another. Alix Shulman expresses these feelings very well, "There are actually laws on the books in most states that define as 'unnatural' and therefore criminal any (sexual) position other than that of the woman on the bottom and the man on the top; laws that make oral sex a crime, though for some women it is the only way of achieving orgasm with another person; laws that make homosexuality a crime, though for some people it is the only acceptable way of loving."[7] These laws should be repealed, not necessarily because you personally may want to participate in these activities, but so that people who do will have the freedom to do so with others who feel similarly inclined. Whether or not you want to experiment with any of the aforementioned possibilities is up to you. For some women trying sexual innovations may be like walking a tightrope; you have to follow your instincts and sense of adventure without shaking the rope so hard that you fall off. Once aware of your own internalized limits, you may find that moving slowly in new areas can allow for greater success and pleasure.

14: Sex and Pregnancy:
Menopause and Aging

The female reproductive system is far more complex than the male's. Many changes occur, of course, during puberty, and also, women have to adapt to monumental physical changes during pregnancy. Then when a woman's reproductive organs are no longer functioning, she goes through the discomforts initiated by the hormonal changes of menopause. During these periods a woman is still a sexual creature, but the changes occurring within her body, which in turn profoundly affect her state of mind, her sense of security, and her happiness, may also have a profound effect upon her sexuality.

Sexuality during pregnancy has only been sparsely researched to date. For the most part, expectant mothers have been treated as asexual beings; for example, many physicians routinely discourage or forbid intercourse and other sexual activities for periods as long as three months—six weeks before delivery and six weeks after. The changes occurring during pregnancy can affect sexuality, but like other aspects of sexuality, these changes are individual and each woman requires individual treatment.

Research conducted on pregnancy and sexuality generally divides the nine-month gestation period into three trimesters. Masters and Johnson's[1] research on one hundred one pregnant women, and the more recent research by Solberg, Butler, and Wagner[2] on two hundred sixty women, indicate a general loss of sexual desire by women during the first trimester. Of course, there are exceptions; some women are even more erotically inclined. For instance, the irritation caused by the pressure of the uterus on the bladder, and hence the urethra, caused Dana to experience increased sexuality. But in general, possibly because of the fatigue and nausea that sometimes accompanies the early months of pregnancy, many women tend to lose interest in sex. In the early months of pregnancy, women frequently complain also of severe and

152

uncomfortable breast tenderness during sexual excitation.[3] Another reason cited by many women for cutting back on sexual activity is fear of injury to the fetus during intercourse. It is true that women with a history of miscarriage during the first trimester should refrain from sexual activities, including masturbation, but if this history is not present and there is no abdominal pain or bleeding, there is generally no physical reason why she should not enjoy sexual activities if she wants to. However, since pregnancy often causes a real physical drain on the woman's body, some women just may not have the energy to be sexually active, especially if they have other children to care for or a job commitment to fulfill.

Masters and Johnson, and Solberg et al. differ in their research conclusions as regards sexual desire during the second trimester. Masters and Johnson found there frequently was an increased sexual drive, sometimes even surpassing pre-pregnancy levels;[4] the Solberg study found a general decrease in desire for intercourse, and also for masturbation and oral-genital sex, possibly indicating that the loss of sexual interest may not be due solely to the physical discomfort of intercourse.[5] However, in both studies, exceptions to the general trend were apparent, indicating again the highly individualistic relationship between pregnancy and sex.[6] For example, Tina, who during her fourth and fifth months had no interest in partner sex and who experienced considerable discomfort with intercourse, found that her desire for masturbation and frequency of masturbation increased markedly.

Masters and Johnson noted some physiological differences in the sexual response cycle between pregnant and nonpregnant women. First, lubrication generally develops more rapidly and in greater quantity when a woman is pregnant.[7] Orgasms tend to be as satisfying or more so during the second stage of pregnancy and it is not uncommon for women to become orgasmic, or multiply orgasmic, for the first time, during and/or after pregnancy.[8] This change may be the result of the increased vascularity in the pelvic area that develops to nourish the fetus.[9]

Because of the increased vascularity, and increased blood supply to the pelvis, the area can become very congested during sexual excitement—as a consequence, even though the woman experiences a satisfying orgasm, the physical contractions may be so diminished in intensity that orgasm fails to resolve sexual tension completely. Therefore, the resolution phase may take a considerable period of time.[10]

During the last trimester of pregnancy, Solberg et al. again find decreased sexual activity and decreased frequency of orgasm resulting from coitus.[11] This effect may be due to the discomfort of an advanced pregnancy or the awkwardness of coitus as well as the fear of injuring the fetus or causing a premature birth.[12] Or it could be the result of learned expectations that sex should be discontinued during this period.

Sexual activity during the last six weeks or month of pregnancy appears to be the major point of controversy. Masters and Johnson[13] and The Sex Information and Education Council of the United States (SIECUS)[14] agree that decisions about sexual abstinence should be made in an individualized manner, with the advice of a physician. There has been no real evidence that orgasms occurring during the last trimester cause premature births.[15] The consensus is that there is no reason for abstinence from sexual activities during the last months of pregnancy for any reason other than the woman's own physical discomfort, providing that she is free of pelvic or abdominal pain, uterine bleeding, ruptured membranes which can cause infection to mother and child, actual labor, and individual problems accompanying the last weeks of pregnancy.[16] In the case of individual problems, a physician may require abstinence from all sexual activity which leads to orgasm—including masturbation. If intercourse is thought to be unwise, check with your physician to see whether other sexual activities are permissible.

Some women use doctors' orders to legitimate their lack of desire, a lack which is totally normal and frequently felt by pregnant women, and a lack which really requires no justification. The extensive physical and hormonal changes occurring during pregnancy are highly individual, and each woman responds according to her over-all physical and psychological make-up. There is no "normal" response. Some women desire sex more often than before pregnancy and some less often. Some find it more satisfying and some less so. Solbert et al. indicate, however, that the lack of desire is more likely to occur in women who do not normally experience orgasm with partner sexual activity.[17]

The woman's behavior is not the only cause for reduced sexual activity. The male partner may lose sexual interest during his partner's pregnancy. Common reasons include concern for the expectant mother's physical comfort, fear of injuring the fetus, and sometimes aversion to the physical appearance of the pregnant woman.[18] It is important for male partners to be aware of the tremendous physiological drain of pregnancy, and also of the mental preparations for child-rearing which may be diminishing the woman's sexual interest. In general, however, her need for intimacy and caring, if not sex, is often greater during this period than at other times.

During the advanced stages of pregnancy and the early post-partum period, it is helpful to keep in mind many of the previously mentioned non-coital techniques and positions which can be used for more pleasurable, and less awkward and uncomfortable, sexual activity. The woman astride position, the "X"-shaped position, and all the rear entry positions can help to alleviate discomfort. Manual stimulation can provide an excellent means for achieving sexual release if orgasm is not prohibited by your physician. Oral sex is too, provided that no air is blown into the vagina, because air bubbles entering the uterus during pregnancy can cause an embolism which may prove fatal to the fetus and the mother.[19]

The important thing to realize is that you can continue to be sexual if you want to be so long as your physician finds no concrete reasons to prohibit sexual activity. Having a couple refrain totally from sexual activity during a period in which both are going through considerable changes and may really desire and require the intimacy that sex provides may put an unnecessary strain on the partners and on the relationship.

Authorities also disagree about the need for a lengthy period of sexual abstinence after birth. It depends upon the individual woman's situation, her level of sexual desire, and especially her rate of healing and recovery from the delivery.[20] Bleeding should have ceased, although a brownish discharge may persist and can often be disregarded.[21] Unfortunately, the sexual structures are often damaged by careless obstetrical handling and many women unnecessarily experience lasting pain with intercourse as the result. Practicing the Kegel exercises can promote healing and tightening of the vagina after delivery. Sex after childbirth can return to normal fairly quickly and nursing often assists the recovery process. Women generally tend to experience more intense and satisfying orgasms after their first pregnancy and this change appears to be permanent.[22]

The research of Masters and Johnson indicates that nursing mothers show a more rapid return to being sexually interested than non-nursing mothers.[23] The rapid revival of sexual interest suggests that nursing may promote more rapid recovery because of the accompanying uterine contractions; these contractions may help stop the bleeding and help return the uterus to its normal state more quickly.[24] Some sensual-sexual feelings can accompany the act of nursing. Some women have experienced orgasm while nursing their infant.[25] In the past many women have felt guilty or abnormal because of these sensuous feelings.[26]

One problem is that women are made to feel embarrassed about nursing, embarrassed to expose a breast in public, embarrassed if the nursing feels pleasurable, and especially embarrassed because someone may accuse her of doing it for "sexual kicks," if nursing is continued past early infancy.

Despite prevailing folk wisdom, it should be noted that nursing is not a dependable contraceptive even though it can, in many cases, retard ovulation for a considerable period of time. Some birth control method should be instituted immediately after the child's birth if pregnancy is not desired right away.

Sexual activity in the advancing years is another common source of concern for women. However, sex at that time of life need not pose a difficulty for women. Many women find that their sexual appetite increases as they get older. Kinsey and Masters and Johnson found that althought men attain their peak of sexual responsiveness at about age eighteen, women don't reach their sexual peak until their late thirties and early forties.[27] There are several possible reasons for the relatively late occurrence of the sexual peak in women: the elimination of the concern about becoming pregnant, of child-rearing, the slower response of an aging partner who may need more time to develop an erection and reach orgasm, which affords the woman greater sexual pleasure. Also, the increased time and energy available to the couple for sexual activity, especially after retirement.[28]

Menopause also can be a time of considerable mental conflict as well as physical discomfort for many women. Not only do changes in the woman's hormone balance make it obvious that her reproductive years are over, but these changes may make her feel as if her youth has ended and with it her femininity, attractiveness, and desirability as a sexual partner.

However, being older and experienced and without the responsibility of children can give a woman a new-found freedom to continue to explore and grow. Aging need not bring a decline in spirit, but a spirit tempered by experience. The pace may be slower, but the enjoyment need not be less.

Our culture's emphasis on youth and beauty causes older women an unnecessary insecurity. Darlene was nearing fifty and still found her husband very sexy, his slight paunch notwithstanding. He found her equally desirable, but she feared that her sexual drive would lessen after menopause; although she enjoyed being affectionate she was so afraid that she would soon lose her sexual interest that she avoided the whole issue by getting out of bed first in the morning or avoiding sex in other ways in order not to confront what she thought was inevitable. In the group, we simply corrected this misapprehension. Now she is responding more and even initiating sex and is delighted to find that she enjoys it as much as before. It was only her fear that she would not be sexual as she grew older that diminished her enjoyment—not the physiological fact of aging. According to Masters and Johnson, as women age, lubrication may be diminished and slower in developing and the intensity and duration of the physiological response may be reduced. But other problems can be helped by hormone therapy and by continued, regular sexual activity.[29]

Unfortunately, the normal slowing down of sexual responses in both the older man and woman may affect a man's feeling of masculinity. As a result, his desire for sex may decrease as he sees his erection forming more slowly and with less firmness.[30] However, sexual activity need not cease or even radically diminish as a man ages. If he is slow to reach erection, he can stimulate his partner manually and orally and the couple can continue to indulge in mutually satisfying sexual activity. As a matter of fact, pleasure may increase for both since more time is needed for caressing and stimulating each other in order to attain high levels of excitement. Besides, the experience of orgasm is not essential to the enjoyment of sex play. Many older couples are capable of enjoying sex that does not result in orgasm each time.[31] It only seems fair that a slow relaxed enjoyment of sex should be one of the benefits of growing older.

Women undergoing menopausal changes often find the fatigue, irritability, headaches, hot flashes, and nervousness that accompany menopause[32] enough of a drain to make them lose interest in sex. Hormone therapy can reduce these discomforts and help to re-establish sexual interest. In even later years, estrogen and progesterone treatment can help relieve pain in the uterus resulting from orgasmic contractions. It can also help make intercourse less painful. Pain in the vagina and urethra sometimes results from lack of estrogen. This deficiency causes the vaginal walls to become thin, providing less protection for the bladder and urethra during intercourse and thus causing a burning sensation and frequently the need to urinate following intercourse. Also, a lack of hormones reduces the expansibility of the vagina which may make accommodating the penis uncomfortable. Surgical jelly can be helpful in supplying lubrication, and hormone replacement therapy may be desirable to correct or ease the other discomforts.[33]

However, the best preventative for sexual discomfort as we age is an active sex life including both masturbation and/or intercourse. Masters and Johnson found that women who engaged in intercourse on the average of once or twice a week had little difficulty producing sufficient lubrication and experienced little or no discomfort with sex as compared to women with a less active sex life.[34] However, it is also important to recognize the reaction of many older women who may have never or only rarely enjoyed sex and who may be thoroughly relieved finally to be able to use menopause, a hysterectomy, or old age as a reason to avoid it altogether.

One perplexing problem that faces many older women who desire sexual activity is a lack of available sexual partners. Because women live longer than men, they are more likely to find themselves without sexual partners in later years. One eighty-seven-year-old great-grandmother asked me what she could do about her considerable sex drive since she had no current sexual partner. For her and other older women in similar situations, self-stimulation can be very important in providing a regular and satisfying release of sexual tensions.

15: Your Responsibility to Your Body

While this book specifically addresses itself to sexuality, it is in essence speaking to the larger subject of how women can take responsibility for themselves. Being responsible for oneself includes taking care of one's general health, and the health of one's organs.

The information in this chapter is not new. The media are constantly bombarding us with messages urging preventative health measures, but we frequently don't heed these messages—sometimes because we don't really consider ourselves important enough to take adequate health precautions.

For example, taking care not to get pregnant if you don't want a child is of supreme importance. Birth control is now relatively easy, and readily and inexpensively available in this country through the county public health services and Planned Parenthood as well as other local sources—yet many women are seeking abortions for unplanned pregnancies.

Abortions are safer and more easily obtained today than ever before, but for some women they do cause considerable mental anguish. Birth control methods all seem to have their drawbacks, but generally speaking, they are probably more acceptable than an unwanted pregnancy or sexual abstinence. *Our Bodies Ourselves* by the Boston Women's Health Book Collective gives an excellent description and sensitive presentation of the various birth control methods, providing information on how they work, their complications or drawbacks, and where they can be obtained.[1] You might refer to that book if you are considering birth control for the first time or if you are dissatisfied with your present contraceptive method and desire a change.

Being aware of venereal disease is especially important for any sexually active female. Contrary to myth, "nice girls" do get VD. Venereal disease attacks males and females of all ages and of all social classes. One should be as alert to the dangers

159

of VD as to the dangers of any other disease. Sexual contact with a partner who harbors the disease is all that is needed for exposure. If you suspect that you have been exposed, see your doctor or visit a clinic. Also, a VD check should be part of every routine physical, but it is not, so you may need to specifically request it. The symptoms of gonorrhea are often mild, brief, or inconspicuous and many women experience no symptoms whatsoever. This is particularly disturbing since VD has reached epidemic proportions. Gonorrhea "is the most common among significant infectious diseases in the United States."[2] Chancre sores on the genitals, mouth sores, vaginal discharge, or flu-like symptoms, which may appear briefly and then disappear, can be some of the warning signals of VD. The disappearance of any of the symptoms does not mean the end of the disease. Gonorrhea can cause sterility or can infect a fetus; syphilis, in advanced stages, can cause seriout damage such as blindness, insanity, paralysis and death.

The chapter on VD in *Our Bodies Ourselves* stresses the importance of obtaining VD cultures at VD clinics or physicians' offices if you have any reason to believe you may have been exposed to the disease.[3] A blood test is given for syphilis. For diagnosis of gonorrhea a gram-stain test as well as cultures from both the cervix and rectum or urethra are necessary since gonorrhea often is not identifiable by culture, even when the woman has the disease. Treatment is simple, generally through oral or intravenous doses of penicillin or penicillin substitutes. *Two* negative blood tests taken several weeks apart are recommended after treatment for syphilis, to make sure that the infection has been cleared up; *two* negative culture tests for gonorrhea are recommended to make sure that it has been cured. It is your responsibility, and you are the one to suffer, if you don't insist on adequate tests. If you fail to do so, you may find out, days, months, or possibly years later, that you are still infected and that the disease has done irreparable harm.

Anyone who has VD is responsible for notifying everyone with whom he or she has had recent sexual contact so that they can obtain testing and, if infected, treatment. Reporting contacts is a major step toward controlling the spread of VD; there are no vaccines to protect us. Such vaccines are needed, but little has been done to develop them, in part because our culture has assumed that VD is a punishment for those who insist upon what society considers "immoral sexual contact" (more than one sexual partner). Until more money is spent on education, research, and preventative treatment, it is more important than ever for everyone to protect themselves through regular checkups. Washing the genitals with soap and water before sexual contact can help protect against transmitting the infection. Urinating after intercourse may help. But these measures in themselves do not afford reliable protection. Condoms provide the best protection available from contracting VD through intercourse. Recent research in Sweden indicates that a rise in condoms sold correlates with a decline in cases of gonorrhea.[4] For further information about VD, your local public health service, community pharmacist, family planning agency, physican, school nurse, or free VD clinic should be contacted.

Vaginal infections are a very common source of discomfort for many women. The most common vaginal infections are yeast infections and trichomoniasis. Vaginal infections sometimes cause itching or burning. Yeast infections often result from unusual emotional stress, contraceptive pills, antibiotics, or excessive douching, all of which can alter the natural pH of the vagina, thereby providing the already present bacteria with a more conducive environment in which to thrive. Inserting yogurt into the vagina or a mildly acidic douche (two tablespoons of white vinegar to one quart warm water) can alleviate the problem, but if it persists, simple medical treatment consisting of vaginal suppositories is generally effective. If yeast infections recur, it might be beneficial to wear cotton instead of nylon underpants and not to wear clothes that are tightly fitted in the crotch area. Or, a change of the method of contraception, of diet, or of factors in your emotional environment may be in order.

Trichomoniasis can be transmitted through intercourse. It can be treated by prescribed medication and any male partner should be treated as well.

Vaginal infections are not generally as serious as venereal disease, but often can be even more uncomfortable. They should be attended to promptly.

Taking care of your sexual organs includes a yearly pap smear, a painless procedure to check for uterine cancer. This test should be done at least once a year, or more frequently if any irregular cells are found as a result of the test. Uterine cancer is not uncommon, but if diagnosed early, less severe procedures than a hysterectomy (the removal of the uterus and possibly other reproductive organs) are possible, and the chance that the cancer will spread to other organs is greatly reduced. Through a regular and painless checkup an untimely death can be prevented.

In addition to seeing your doctor for a once-a-year checkup, you must be responsible for examining your breasts every month. Don't wait for your physician to check your breasts only once a year. Lie on your back, lift your right arm over your head and examine the right breast thoroughly with your left hand. Massage the whole area deeply with circular motions. Reverse the position to examine the left breast. When you first begin to check your breasts, the natural and normal masses in your breasts may scare you and you may fear you have breast cancer, but self-examination of the breasts following each period, when the breasts are less grainy and lumpy, will familiarize you with the normal masses; then when an abnormal lump appears, you can have it immediately checked by a doctor. Only a small percentage of unusual breast lumps are cancerous. If you let a lump go too long and it is malignant, the cancerous cells can infect the lymphatic system and spread to other organs of your body. If discovered and treated early, the lump can be treated or removed. At worst, a breast may have to be removed. Ignoring a lump will not make it go away. As difficult and scary as it is to face the possibility of having breast or uterine cancer, especially if it runs in your family, it is still essential to have these things checked.

Both women and men have a tendency to ignore or neglect medical problems which often become more severe the longer they are left untended. Some of us ignore our medical problems because we fear they might be serious. Others do so because they have received treatment by physicans in the past that makes them dread a physical and especially a pelvic exam, as a potentially disagreeable and humiliating experience. Unfortunately, many doctors are insensitive to the discomfort a woman feels, with her feet in stirrups and her crotch in full view. It seems, though, that the more exams we get the more we realize how routine it is for the doctor and the less embarrassing it is for us. However, if your physician uses cold speculums for pelvic examinations, despite your requests to warm them, or treats you harshly or disrespectfully by all means change doctors. Don't let discomfort with a doctor cause you to procrastinate about getting regular checkups.

Finding a competent doctor you like is extremely important, but often not easy. Gynecologists frequently disagree among themselves about appropriate treatment. I could cite hundreds of medical horror stories, breast lumps ignored, unnecessary hysterectomies in young women. Find a physician you trust—male or female—neither is necessarily infallible, and receive regular medical checkups. Check on potential problems immediately. Make certain you understand what is happening. Demand information. Don't accept a hasty dismissal. If you don't feel comfortable about the exam, or the doctor's diagnosis, or the treatment suggested, you have every right to another medical opinion. Millions of women deny the existence of physical ailments which only become worse over time. No one wants to be considered a complainer or a hysteric who gets excited about the least little thing. You may feel embarrassed if you consult a doctor and turn out to be *well* instead of dying. Also, it's natural to want to believe that there is nothing wrong, so we disregard our fears. However, it is important to complain when it comes to our physical health, for if we don't no one else will.

Our lives are essentially our responsibility.

16: Bringing up Children Sexually

Many women in the groups were concerned about what they could do so that their children, particularly their daughters, would not grow up with the same inhibitions and misconceptions about sex that had taken so much energy to reverse in themselves. Few good books have been written about the sexual education of children. Material is available carefully detailing how to explain reproductive matters and at what age information is appropriate, but very little has been researched or written about how to deal with children's natural curiosity about sexual matters. However, three books have been recently written by Dr. Wardell Pomeroy on the subject: *Girls and Sex*, *Boys and Sex*, and *Your Child and Sex*.

Self-exploration is a natural part of the developmental process, and this includes a child's exploration of bodies—the mother's body, the father's body, friends' bodies, and the child's own body.

How would we have liked to have been brought up sexually so that we were less inhibited and more sensual and sexual? How can we change things so our children can have a better experience? Child-rearing is an individual matter and something with which each mother and father has to struggle. Perhaps this discussion will present a few options for you to explore further in your family.

All too frequently, children have been treated as innocent asexual beings. But children most certainly are not asexual. All the sexual organs capable of providing pleasure are present, and children are sexual creatures, from birth. Theirs is not the same sexuality we know as adults, but it is nonetheless sexuality. The baby playing with your breast is at least sensual if not sexual. The two-year-old who seductively crawls into bed between Mommy and Daddy is sexual, although not with the same explicit sexual intent of an adult. The five-year-old girl, who dresses up and sits on her father's lap kissing him and asking him if he will marry her when she grows up, is sexual. The seven-year-old who is masturbating, possibly even to orgasm, is sexual. The eight-year-old prancing around without any clothes on is sexual. These are children passing through learning stages on the way to becoming adult sexual beings. Some of their behavior represents a mimicking of Mommy or Daddy and some results from natural bodily curiosity but it is all sexual though not necessarily with the adult's awareness of what sexuality means.

A major problem in dealing with sexuality in children has been the adult's own embarrassment and discomfort with sex. There has been a tendency to ignore children's sexual questions and gestures, a tendency to believe that an adult doesn't have to answer sexual questions because the child couldn't possibly know what she is asking. This denies the child's sexuality because of the adult's own uneasiness. The result, of course, is that the child gets the message that she is asking improper questions that her mother doesn't like to hear, so the child's tendency is to stop risking her mother's anger, keep quiet, and wonder silently to herself. Meanwhile, the child feels embarrassment, shame, and remains ignorant about sex, and many reach adulthood to experience excessive sexual inhibitions, the absence of orgasm, or the experience of an unwanted pregnancy.

A number of my colleagues, informed in the area of sex and child-rearing, advocate open, honest, direct dealing with sexual questions or sexual curiosity in children. They feel this is the best method. The child should be given information, with the parent frequently asking questions to determine if the child understood, if she has any further questions, if the information disturbed or upset her, so the parent can correct any misconceptions from the beginning.

The biggest obstacle is dealing with issues that are not quite resolved in the parent's own mind, while still trying to be honest. One mother accepted masturbation intellectually, but found the old fears and feelings of disgust or shame were evoked when her son played with his penis. She did not want to alarm him by forbidding him to touch himself, but she knew he would detect her discomfort if she told him that what he was doing was fine, while she was feeling otherwise. Children pick up mixed messages quickly and respond with confusion. They realize something is wrong, although they may not be quite sure exactly what. A parent's attempt to in-form the child of more than one prevailing intellectual opinion while also directly expressing personal discomfort may be one way of dealing with unsettled issues. In that way at least the child knows exactly why a parent is uncomfortable. This particular woman said, "I know it feels good to play with your penis and it's OK, but it makes me uncomfortable when you do it here in the living room. I would feel much better if you would go in to your bedroom where you can have privacy."

It is important for children to know that touching one's sexual organs is supposed to feel good—that other people touch themselves and have similar sensations and the response is not abnormal or shameful; that sometimes a special feeling called orgasm can occur, but it doesn't always so they shouldn't feel abnormal when it happens, or ignorant if it doesn't. It might be a good idea to say that the feelings are good feelings and should be enjoyed but possibly only in the privacy of one's own room, and when others aren't around. There are special rooms for many activities (kitchen, bathroom, etc.). Children are able to understand this.

The issue is a touchy one—to be able to give your children positive sex messages and open the home to sexual questions when you don't feel totally comfortable about it yourself. To give one's children experiences different from one's own, however, is a valid goal.

Physical contact is essential for children. Studies show that children in orphanages who received adequate nourishment but were not held, cuddled, kissed, and caressed would often become ill.[1] But in our culture it is frequently customary to discontinue physical contact as the child grows older, especially with sons. Then after marriage, miraculously, the two people who have been denied physical contact for years are supposed to be able to respond physically and emotionally without inhibitions—which was natural for them as a child, but was trained out of them as they grew older. Many of us grew up in families where touching was prohibited and so we tend to maintain a distance from our children. Others of us may find ourselves sexually turned on by our children, and these impulses may frighten us so much that we maintain physical distance in an effort to avoid the unacceptable sexual feelings and possibly even to protect our children from being the object of our sexual fantasies.

Sexual feelings for our children begin early. It is important to realize that sexual fantasies about one's children are normal. Many mothers in the groups reported having some such fantasies at least occasionally. Children are sexual, warm, cuddly human beings—we can feel turned on and have the fantasies but we don't have to act them out. Acting them out can be detrimental to the child, while just having the fantasy is perfectly harmless.

One of the group members, Samantha, had sexual fantasies about her five-year-old step-daughter who was going through a very seductive stage. Samantha was afraid she might actually try to seduce the child and as a result picked fights with her to keep them physically apart, hoping this would prevent her from acting out her worst fears. Their relationship was getting worse and worse. Another woman in the group announced that she, too, had had sexual fantasies which included her four-year-old daughter. She would use the fantasies during masturbation and found that after about two months her fantasies began naturally to include activities and people other than her daughter. So it was suggested that Samantha allow herself to have the fantasies, to exaggerate them, and carry them, still in fantasy, to the greatest possible extreme. Samantha returned the next week to say that she had followed our advice and actively fantasized sexual situations which included her step-daughter; she found that not only did she not act on them, but she felt closer to her step-daughter and could allow herself to be more affectionate and caring with the child. To her amazement she tired of the fantasies and soon replaced them with more interesting ones. She also found that she wasn't jealous of the daughter's seductive behavior toward the child's father any more.

Accurate information is important to curious youngsters. If your relationship is a close and caring one, and your child trusts you and feels comfortable with you, she will look to you for guidance and answers—especially in the early years. During adolescence things may change because of the adolescent's intense need for privacy and rebellion in order to establish herself as her own person. But if your relationship has been open until then, she should have received the necessary and important information about sexuality before this difficult and conflicted time.

Information need not exceed the limits of the child's question. A child asks a question, but we may not be aware of exactly what it is she wishes to have explained. Seeing the world through a child's eyes, and knowing exactly what she wants to know, can be very hard for an adult. A good way to find out precisely what is confusing the child, which in turn will make it far easier to answer her question, is to ask what *she* thinks about it or how *she* thinks it works. This can radically simplify a seemingly all-encompassing question. For example, one three-and-a-half-year-old asked Diane, "How does a car work?" Diane's mind immediately raced to all the complexities of a combustion engine, most of which she really didn't understand herself. But before she jumped in over both their heads, Diane asked, "How do *you* think it works?" "Well, I *don't* think you push it with your feet," the child answered. This greatly simplified Diane's problem as she explained the absolute rudiments of a motor attached to the wheels which causes the car to move. If the child wants more information, she will usually ask further questions. Generally, children hear only as much as they are prepared to hear at a particular point in time and walk away when they become anxious or burdened with information they cannot handle. Always asking if the child understands or has further questions or is upset by something you have said can help weed out the child's misconceptions and keep disturbing information from festering within.

Using diagrams and pictures can sometimes clarify things, or just using words that a child will not misinterpret. A friend of mine was told at the age of five that babies came from an egg in Mommy's tummy that Daddy fertilized. For years she carried around the mental image of Daddy shoveling manure on a chicken egg sitting on Mommy's tummy.

Information about sex is generally met by children with embarrassment and giggles—especially at the beginning. Their reaction may make it even more difficult for us to sensitively answer their questions if we feel they are not serious or are ridiculing us, especially when we are already experiencing discomfort and yet are trying to deal with the issue. It is important to remember that children may pick up our discomfort or may already be aware that this is a private subject and feel awkward and uneasy discussing it even though they are starved for accurate information. However, as you begin to address their questions, children will generally quiet down and listen attentively.

There is no reason to keep children from knowing that sex is an enjoyable, pleasurable activity; that sex is for fun first and for babies second. It makes no sense to hide the physical side of a loving relationship. It is important for children to see their parents embrace, kiss, cuddle, and in general act affectionately toward one another. However, in our culture, this does not mean making love with the children as spectators or participants, though two- to four-year-olds have a fantastic ability to open unlocked doors at precisely the wrong moments. It might be good to let your child know that you and Daddy make love in the privacy of your bedroom; that during that time you don't like to be disturbed and any questions and problems can generally wait until afterward. To treat sex with dignity and love rather than to shroud it in awkward and unspeakable mystery is an excellent way of instilling a child with a healthy attitude toward sex.

The pleasure sex provides can be acknowledged rather than ignored. Young girls and boys can be told about a girl's clitoris just as they are told about a boy's penis, so that when they accidently discover this tiny but pleasurable organ, they don't feel like freaks. Alix Shulman wrote a lovely dialogue about explaining the difference between boys and girls:

BOY: What's the difference between boys and girls?
MOTHER: Mainly their sex organs. A boy has a penis and a girl has a clitoris.
BOY: What's a clitoris?
MOTHER: It's a tiny sensitive organ on a girl's body about where a penis is on a boy's body. It feels good to touch, like your penis. . . .
BOY: What's it for?
MOTHER: For making love, for pleasure. When people love each other, one of the ways they show it is by caressing one another's bodies, including their sex organs.
BOY: How do girls pee?
MOTHER: There's an opening below the clitoris for peeing. A man uses his penis for peeing, for making love, and for starting babies. Women have three separate places for these. . . . (and so on . . .)[2]

Children are innocent and curious. They know no guilt until others instill it in them and sometimes it happens without parents even noticing. Sarah walked in on her four-and-a-half-year-old daughter while she was masturbating and the child began to cry hysterically. She hated herself because she did this and didn't want her mother to see and made her mother promise not to tell anyone. Sarah had no idea how her daugher got these negative feelings at such a young age. She could not remember ever telling her child that it was bad to touch herself.

This illustration makes it only too clear how little control we actually have over what a child hears and sees outside the home. Unless given permission and positive messages about sex from their parents, society, religion, schools, friends, and relatives all too quickly instill negative sex messages. Positive and accepting statements about sex, as opposed to the old oppressive messages, might ultimately improve the child's attitude and approach to sex. Landis et al. found that catching a child in the act of masturbation or making threatening statements about the act induces guilt, but has no effect on the frequency of masturbation. The child will continue to masturbate, but will also feel guilty about it.[3] Also, Kinsey's research indicates that a better sexual-orgasmic adjustment to marriage is more probable if the girl has experienced orgasm, by whatever means, prior to marriage.[4] These are good reasons not to discourage a child's masturbation.

Children's sexual exploration is like all other areas of exploration. For the child it is a way of learning about her environment and how to make a place for herself within it. Exploration includes urinating while standing up like a boy, wearing make-up like mother, playing doctor with other boys and girls down the street, and exploring sexual feelings with a girlfriend. Physical and loving relationships between two or more girls or two or more boys is a very common and natural part of the growing up process. It does not mean that the child is heterosexual, homosexual, or bisexual. Each child will have the chance to choose a sexual orientation later on in life. This experimentation is a part of the development process for many children and not a cause for alarm or worry. One should try not to have the child feel abnormal or ashamed about the expression of budding sexual feelings.

Perhaps the most important source of feelings toward sexuality and about a girl's own body comes from messages from her mother. If a mother approaches life positively and freely shares her enthusiasm and love, if she holds aspirations for her daughters which move beyond the confines of traditional roles, then it is likely that the child will develop in a less inhibited, more optimistic, self-sufficient, and independent way.

17: Personal Liberation

What if you have assumed responsibility for your sexuality and followed the exercises in this book diligently, and still experience no progress in attaining sexual satisfaction? Hopefully, you are enjoying sex more now, even if you aren't orgasmic yet. However, what can you do now? One alternative is to begin the program a second time, especially if your first attempt was unsystematic. Beth's experience illustrates what one can do on one's own. A month after the group ended, Beth wrote: "Though my sexual responses are far from secure, I did climax recently while being pleasured by Lee! This is a big first, the goal I had just about given up achieving. This, though I don't understand how it happened, tells me I'm on the right track. I will continue the exercises and homework as faithfully as possible, on the assumption that it was these things which led me to my initial success."

Still, even with time, the tools contained in this book may not be totally sufficient to help you realize your sexual potential. But don't despair. If you have a clitoris, you can have an orgasm (except in extremely rare circumstances) but you may require outside assistance from someone who can help you with individual difficulties. Or, you may want to get a physical exam if you suspect any medical difficulties. Sometimes a friend who is compassionate, or a small group of women friends who are open to discussing the intimate details of their sex lives sensitively together can be very helpful. However, finding such confidantes may or may not be possible in your community. Joining a woman's group which is specifically oriented toward sexual problems, which is led by an experienced female sex therapist, may be an ideal solution, but, again, such programs may not be available in your area. However, more and more reputable sex therapy programs are becoming available.[1] The advantage to all of these options where women are working with other women is that it gives

171

the woman an opportunity to see that she is not alone in her sexual difficulties; second, the women can learn from each other by sharing experiences and by developing more alternatives and solutions to problems than they might have been able to do individually; and third, and most important, a group of women working together can provide a significant measure of support for one another while each member is attempting to make changes. Women working closely together and sharing intimately can create a very powerful force.

Some women may find that it is necessary to change some aspects of their relationship with a partner, in order to become orgasmic. Both people may need to develop additional skills in communicating; or receive help in learning to express feelings more openly. If the man frequently has problems getting or holding an erection, or if he ejaculates almost immediately after intercourse begins, it might be best for the couple to seek sex or marital counseling together. Receiving counseling together is important if the sexual problem is indicative of other problems in the relationship and therefore cannot be treated as an isolated problem, or by working with only one partner.

This book, and the women's therapy groups, are both about liberation in the most basic sense: liberation from the social scripting which prevents women (and men, though perhaps in different ways) from taking control of their lives and expressing themselves as complete and autonomous individuals—free to act the way they feel despite the expectations of others.

Sexual liberation entails acceptance of your own unique sexual responses and sexuality in general, not because it conforms to external standards or solely because it provides pleasure for a partner, but because it is an intimate expression of yourself.

Being sexually liberated means the freedom to choose—to choose the kind of stimulation that works for you; to choose the sexual activities that are pleasurable for you. It also means being free to choose *not* to do things that fail to meet your needs or values. Being sexually liberated means having in harmony your beliefs, feelings, actions, and desires about your own sexuality.

Sexual liberation is one aspect of personal liberation. Taking control of your life, at the most intimate, personal, and fundamental level—the level of your sexuality—seems to lead to extending control over other areas of life. The women in the groups not only became orgasmic, but, in many cases, found new jobs, terminated unsatisfactory relationships, and initiated new relationships. In general, they became more assertive in having their needs, both sexual and nonsexual, met. They became more self-assured and felt far better about themselves and their bodies.

Once we feel better about ourselves, once we assume that we have rights that deserve respect from others, we are in a position to begin liberating ourselves from the roles society has prescribed. Women's liberation, by freeing women, may in turn free men from their counterpart roles. Such liberation would allow women the freedom to speak, to teach, to be an authority in areas of their own competency. It could thereby free men from having to be experts, allowing them to listen and learn without being threatened. Liberation means having the freedom to be strong and caring of others, while still being able to be open and accepting of care from others. Liberation entails being free to be passive and receiving or to be assertive and giving; to be aggressive or nurturing. And most importantly, being liberated means the freedom to say no, because when you can say no when you want to, you are more free to say yes—and really mean it. Being able to say no makes saying yes a purer pleasure. Being in control of your life means being free to say either.

When you can take control of your life, and feel free to be yourself, when you are personally liberated, you lose fear. Feeling secure within yourself diminishes fear of others, of the unknown, fear of that which is unfamiliar or of those who are different. This diminished fear coupled with a sense of self-respect allows for greater respect of others and their rights to be themselves—each being free and self-determined.

Sexual liberation is a beginning.

NOTES

INTRODUCTION NOTES

1. Hunt (1974), p. 16.
2. Kinsey (1953), p. 22.
3. Hunt (1974), p. 212.
4. Kinsey (1953), p. 408.
5. Personal communication with Hugh Edwards, Director, Research Guild, Inc., Chicago.
6. Hunt (1973), p. 194.
7. Reuben (1969), p. 129.
8. Barbach (in press).
9. Masters and Johnson (1970), pp. 295–316.
10. Lobitz and LoPiccolo (1972), pp. 267–68.
11. Lobitz and LoPiccolo (1972), pp. 267–68.
12. Nelson (1974), pp. 44–45.
13. Kinsey (1953), p. 146, found there is far greater variety sexually among females than among males.

CHAPTER 1 NOTES

1. Personal communication with Dr. Alan Margolis, OB-Gyn., U.C. Medical Center, San Francisco.
2. Masters and Johnson (1966), p. 133.
3. Kleegman (1959), p. 243, Kaplan (1974), p. 32, and Jorgensen (1973), p. 609.
4. Kaplan (1974), p. 32, and Kinsey (1973), p. 371.
7. Kinsey (1953), p. 384.
8. Mead (1949), pp. 218–23.
9. Masters and Johnson (1966), pp. 191–92.
10. Koedt (1971), p. 312.
11. Anderson, Judith, "Everyone Suffers in the Family," San Francisco *Chronicle*, April 15, 1974, p. 15.
12. Hunt (1974), p. 341.
13. O'Connor and Stein

5. Clark and Wallin (1965), p. 134.
6. Ford and Beach (1951), pp. 254–55.

14. Kaplan (1974), p. 71.
15. Sherfey (1973), p. 165.

(1972), p. 165.

CHAPTER 2 NOTES

1. Freud (1965), p. 118.
2. Masters and Johnson (1966), pp. 45–67.
3. Huelsman (in press).
4. Kinsey (1953), p. 542.
5. Young (1964), pp. 169–80.
6. Webster (1966), p. 761.
7. Webster (1966), p. 275.

8. Webster (1966), p. 1607.
9. Ford and Beach (1951), p. 266.
10. Ford and Beach (1951), p. 266.
11. Hunt (1974), pp. 155–56.
12. Hunt (1974), p. 149.

CHAPTER 4 NOTES

1. "J" (1969), p. 97.

CHAPTER 5 NOTES

1. Masters and Johnson (1966), pp. 56–57.
2. Lowry (in press), chapter titled: "Some Issues in the Histology of the Clitoris."
3. Kaplan (1974), p. 28.
4. Masters and Johnson (1966), p. 191.
5. Lowry (in press), chapter titled: "Some Issues in the Histology of the Clitoris."
6. Kegel (1952), pp. 521–24.
7. Personal communication with Dr. Alan Margolis, Ob-Gyn., U.C. Medical Center, San Francisco.

10. Masters and Johnson (1966), p. 45.
11. Kaplan (1974), p. 72.
12. Kinsey (1953), p. 163.
13. Masters and Johnson (1966), pp. 27–170.
14. Masters and Johnson (1966), p. 66.
15. Sherfey (1973), pp. 112–13.
16. Kaplan (1974), pp. 106–08.
17. Kinsey (1973), p. 375.
18. Bergler and Kroger (1954), p. 82.
19. Masters and Johnson (1966), p. 65.
20. Reuben (1969), p. 50.
21. Personal communication

8. Kaplan (1974), p. 441.
9. Netter (1965), p. 3.

with Dr. Len Laskow, Ob-Gyn., U.C. Medical Center, San Francisco.

CHAPTER 6 NOTES

1. Kinsey (1953), pp. 668–69.
2. Kaplan (1974), p. 63.
3. Fisher (1973), p. 280.
4. Kinsey (1953), pp. 670–72.
5. Hunt (1974), p. 24.
6. Schmidt and Sigusch (1973), pp. 117–44.
7. Hunt (1974), pp. 90–93; p. 332.
8. Kinsey (1953), p. 164.
9. Kaplan (1974), pp. 88–89.
10. Kaplan (1974), p. 90.

CHAPTER 7 NOTES

1. Kinsey (1953), p. 133.
2. Kinsey (1953), p. 133.
3. Kinsey (1953), p. 142.
4. Kinsey (1953), p. 132.
5. Kinsey (1953), p. 172.
6. Kinsey (1953), pp. 386–91.
7. Masters and Johnson (1966), p. 133; p. 313.
8. Kinsey (1953), p. 171.
9. Sherfey (1966), p. 144.
10. Gordon (1968), pp. 21–26.
11. Gordon (1968), p. 30.
12. Ford and Beach (1951), p. 155.
13. Kinsey (1953), p. 169.
14. Mead (1949), p. 218.
15. Greenberg (1973), p. 48.
16. Young (1964), p. 170.
17. Kinsey (1953), p. 169.
18. Landis (1940), p. 210.
19. Greenberg (1973), p. 47.
20. Kinsey (1953), p. 170.
21. Hunt (1974), p. 85.
22. Personal communication with Hugh Edwards, Director, Research Guild, Inc., Chicago.
23. Hunt (1974), p. 76.
24. Kinsey (1953), p. 142.
25. Kinsey (1953), p. 132.

CHAPTER 8 NOTES

1. The prelude vibrator is particularly well liked. Vibrator can be obtained through:
Eve's Garden
119 West 57 Street
New York, N. Y. 10019

Sensory Research
5 Laurence Street
Bloomfield, N. J. 07003
Multi Media Resource Center
1525 Franklin Street
San Francisco, Ca. 94109

CHAPTER 9 NOTES

1. Exercises outlined in Rosenberg's *Total Orgasm* have been found beneficial by many women.

2. Martin and Lyon (1972), p. 88.

3. Kinsey (1953), p. 161.

CHAPTER 10 NOTES

1. Koedt (1971), pp. 311–20, Masters and Johnson (1966), p. 66, Sherfey (1966), p. 142, and Kaplan (1974), p. 377.

2. White and Wallach (1973), p. 47.

3. Hunt (1974), p. 20.

4. Moulton (1973), p. 245.

CHAPTER 12 NOTES

1. Masters and Johnson (1970), pp. 71–75.

2. Rosenberg (1973), pp. 170–71.

3. Gebhard (1966), p. 95.

CHAPTER 13 NOTES

1. Hunt (1974), p. 199.
2. Reuben (1969), p. 64.
3. Reuben (1969), pp. 64–65.
4. Kelly, p. 10.

5. Hunt (1974), p. 202.
6. Hunt (1974), p. 36.
7. Shulman (1971), pp. 301–02.

CHAPTER 14 NOTES

1. Masters and Johnson (1966), pp. 156–57.
2. Solberg, Butler, and Wagner (1973), p. 1098.

17. Solberg, Butler, and Wagner (1973), p. 1100.
18. Masters and Johnson (1966), p. 160.

3. Masters and Johnson (1966), p. 143.
4. Masters and Johnson (1966), p. 158.
5. Solberg, Butler, and Wagner (1973), p. 1102.
6. Masters and Johnson (1966), p. 136, and Solberg, Butler, and Wagner (1973), p. 1102.
7. Masters and Johnson (1966), p. 146.
8. Masters and Johnson (1966), p. 159.
9. Sherfey (1972), p. 101.
10. Masters and Johnson (1966), p. 149.
11. Solberg, Butler, and Wagner (1973), p. 1100.
12. Solberg, Butler, and Wagner (1973), p. 1101.
13. Masters and Johnson (1966), p. 168.
14. Israel and Rubin (1967), p. 11.
15. Solberg, Butler and Wagner (1973), p. 1102.
16. Israel and Rubin (1967), p. 10.
19. Personal communication with Dr. Alan Margolis, Ob-Gyn., U.C. Medical Center, San Francisco.
20. Masters and Johnson (1966), p. 167.
21. Israel and Rubin (1967), p. 13.
22. Sherfey (1972), p. 101.
23. Masters and Johnson (1966), p. 163.
24. Brecher (1966), p. 90.
25. Pomeroy (1974), p. 33.
26. Brecher (1966), p. 92.
27. Kaplan (1974), p. 105.
28. Rubin (1966), p. 261.
29. Masters and Johnson (1966), p. 240.
30. Masters and Johnson (1966), pp. 269–70.
31. Kaplan (1974), p. 114.
32. Boston Women's Health Book Collective (1971), p. 234.
33. Masters and Johnson (1966), p. 240.
34. Masters and Johnson (1966), pp. 240–41.

CHAPTER 15 NOTES

1. Boston Women's Health Book Collective (1971), pp. 106–37.
2. Millar (1974), p. 19.
3. Boston Women's Health Book Collective (1971), pp. 98–105.
4. Juhlin (1974), p. 18.

CHAPTER 16 NOTES

1. Ribble (1944), pp. 621–51.
2. Shulman (1971), p. 293.
3. Landis (1940), p. 210.
4. Kinsey (1953), p. 172.

CHAPTER 17 NOTES

1. For information regarding reputable sex therapists or sex therapy programs in your area, write:

American Association of Marriage and Family Counselors
225 Yale Avenue
Claremont, California 91711
(714) 621–4749

American Association of Sex Educators and Counselors
3422 N Street, N.W.
Washington, D.C.
(202) 965–5834

Society for the Scientific Study of Sex
12 East 41 Street
New York, N.Y. 10017

Sex Information and Education Council of the U.S.
1855 Broadway
New York, N.Y. 10023

Your local American Medical Association or Planned Parenthood offices may also have listings of programs in your area.

BIBLIOGRAPHY

Abbott, Sidney and Love, Barbara. *Sappho Was a Right-On Woman: A Liberated View of Lesbianism.* New York: Stein & Day, 1972.

Bach, George and Deutsch, Ronald M. *Pairing.* New York: Avon Books, 1970.

Bach, George and Wyden, Peter. *The Intimate Enemy: How to Fight Fair in Love and Marriage.* New York: Avon Books, 1968.

Barbach, Lonnie G. "Group Treatment of Pre-Orgasmic Women," *Journal of Sex and Marital Therapy,* v. 1, no. 2, 1975. In Press.

Bardwick, Judith M. *Psychology of Women: A Study of Bio-Cultural Conflict.* New York: Harper & Row, 1971.

Beauvoir, Simone de. *The Second Sex.* New York: Bantam Books, Inc., 1952.

Belliveau, Fred and Richter, Lin. *Understanding Human Sexual Inadequacy.* Boston: Little, Brown & Co., 1970.

Bergler, E. and Kroger, W. S. *Kinsey's Myth of Female Sexuality.* New York: Grune & Stratton, 1954.

The Boston Women's Health Book Collective. *Our Bodies, Ourselves: A Book By and For Women.* New York: Simon & Schuster, 1971, 1973.

Brecher, Ruth and Brecher, Edward, Eds. *An Analysis of Human Sexual Response.* New York: Signet, New American Library, 1966.

Brecher, Ruth and Brecher, Edward. "Sex During and After Pregnancy," *An Analysis of Human Sexual Response.* Brecher, Ruth and Brecher, Edward, Eds. New York: Signet, New American Library, 1966, pp. 88–95.

Brown, D. G. "Female Orgasm and Sexual Inadequacy," *An Analysis of Human Sexual Response.* Brecher, Ruth and Brecher, Edward, Eds. New York: Signet, New American Library, 1966, pp. 125–74.

Chesler, Phyllis. "Patient and Patriarch: Women in the Psychotherapeutic Relationship," *Woman in Sexist Society*. Gornick, Vivian and Moran, Barbara K., Eds. New York: Signet, New American Library, 1971, pp. 362–92.

Clark, Alexander L. and Wallin, Paul. "Women's Sexual Responsiveness and the Duration and Quality of their Marriages," *American Journal of Sociology*, v. 71, 1965, pp. 187–96.

Cleland, John. *Fanny Hill: Memoirs of a Woman of Pleasure*. North Hollywood: Brandon House, 1963.

Clifford, Ruth. Unpublished Doctoral Thesis on Masturbation, Stonybrook, 1973.

Comfort, Alex, Ed. *The Joy of Sex*. New York: Crown Publishers, Inc., 1972.

Dodson, Betty. "Liberating Masturbation," Unpublished Article.

Downing, George. *The Massage Book*. New York: Random House, and Berkeley: The Bookworks, 1972.

Dreifus, Claudia. *Woman's Fate: Raps from a Feminist Consciousness-Raising Group*. New York: Bantam Books, National General Co., 1973.

Farber, Leslie H. "I'm Sorry, Dear," *An Analysis of Human Sexual Response*. Brecher, Ruth and Brecher, Edward, Eds. New York: Signet, New American Library, 1966, pp. 291–312.

Fisher, Seymour. *The Female Orgasm*. New York: Basic Books, Inc., 1973.

Ford, Clellans and Beach, Frank A. *Patterns of Sexual Behavior*. New York: Harper & Row, 1951.

Frankfort, Ellen. *Vaginal Politics*. New York: Bantam Books, National General Co., 1972.

Freud, Sigmund, Trans. and Ed. by Strachey, James. *New Introductory Lectures on Psychoanalysis*. New York: W. W. Norton & Co., Inc., 1965.

Friday, Nancy. *My Secret Garden: Women's Sexual Fantasies*. New York: Pocket Books, 1973.

Gebhard, P. H. "Factors in Marital Orgasm," *The Journal of Social Issues*, v. 22, 1966, pp. 88–95.

Gordon, David Cole. *Self Love*. Baltimore: Penguin Books, Inc., 1968.

Gornick, Vivian and Moran, Barbara K., Eds. *Woman in Sexist Society: Studies in Power and Powerlessness*. New York: Signet, New American Library, 1971.

Greenberg, Jerold S. and Archambault, Francis X. "Masturbation, Self-Esteem and Other Variables," *Journal of Sex Research*, v. 9, no. 1, 1973, pp. 41–51.

Greer, Germaine. *The Female Eunuch*. New York: Bantam Books, National General Co., 1970, 1971.

Herschberger, Ruth. *Adam's Rib*. New York: Pellegrini and Cudahy, 1948.

Hite, Shere, Ed. *Sexual Honesty: By Women For Women*. New York: Warner Paperback Library, 1974.

Horney, Karen. *Female Psychology*. New York: W. W. Norton & Co., Inc., 1967.

Huelsman, Ben R. "An Anthropological View of Clitoral and Other Female Genital Mutilations," *The Clitoris*. Lowry, Thomas and Lowry, Thea S., Eds. St. Louis: Warren H. Green Publishers. In Press.

Hunt, Morton. "Sexual Behavior in the 1970's," *Playboy*, October 1973.

Hunt, Morton. *Sexual Behavior in the 1970's*. Chicago: Playboy Press, 1974.

Israel, Leon and Rubin, Isadore. *Sexual Relations During Pregnancy and the Post-Delivery Period*. New York: SIECUS Publications, 1967.

"J". *The Sensuous Woman*. New York: Dell Publishing Co., Inc., 1969.

Jorgensen, Valerie. "The Gynecologist and the Sexually Liberated Woman," *Obstetrics and Gynecology*, v. 42, no. 4, 1973, pp. 607–12.

Juhlin, Lennart. "Public Information on VD Control in Sweden," *The Practicing Physician Confronts VD*. Proceedings of the Third International Venereal Disease Symposium, New Orleans, La., May 31–June 2, 1973, New York: Science and Medicine Publishing Co., Inc., 1974, pp. 17–18.

Kaplan, Helen Singer. *The New Sex Therapy*. New York: Brunner/ Mazel, 1974.

Kegel, A. H. "Sexual Functions of the Pubococcygeus Muscle," *Western Journal of Surgery*, v. 60, no. 10, 1952, pp. 521–24.

Kelly, Kathy. "Radical Sex Manual," Unpublished Paper.

Kinsey, Alfred C., Pomeroy, Wardell B., Martin, Clyde E., and Gebhard, Paul H. *Sexual Behavior in the Human Female*. New York: Pocket Book, Simon & Schuster, 1953.

Kleegman, Sophia. "Frigidity in Women," *Quarterly Review*

of Surgery, Obstetrics and Gynecology, v. 16, 1959, pp. 243–48.

Koedt, Ann. "The Myth of the Vaginal Orgasm," *Liberation Now.* Babcox, Deborah and Belkin, Madeline, Eds. New York: Dell Publishing Co., 1971, pp. 311–20.

Kronhausen, Phyllis and Kronhausen, Eberhard. *The Sexually Responsive Woman.* New York: Ballantine Books, Inc., 1964.

Lobitz, W. Charles and LoPiccolo, Joseph. "New Methods in the Behavioral Treatment of Sexual Dysfunction," *Journal of Behavior Therapy and Experimental Psychiatry, v.* 3, 1972, pp. 265–71.

Lowry, Thomas P. and Lowry, Thea, S., Eds. *The Clitoris.* St. Louis: Warren H. Green Publishers. In Press.

Lowry, Thomas P. "Some Issues in the Histology of the Clitoris," *The Clitoris.* Lowry, Thomas P. and Lowry, Thea S., Eds. St. Louis: Warren H. Green Publishers. In Press.

Lydon, Susan. "The Politics of Orgasm," *Sisterhood Is Powerful.* Morgan, Robin, Ed. New York: Vintage Books, Random House, 1970, pp. 197–204.

Marmor, Judd. "Changing Patterns of Femininity: Psychoanalytic Implications," *Psychoanalysis and Women.* Miller, Jean Baker, Ed. Baltimore: Penguin Books, Inc., 1973, pp. 221–38.

Martin, Del and Lyon, Phillis. *Lesbian Woman.* New York: Bantam Books, National General Co., 1972.

Masters, William H. and Johnson, Virginia E. *Human Sexual Response.* Boston: Little, Brown & Co., 1966.

Masters, William H. and Johnson, Virginia E. *Human Sexual Inadequacy.* Boston: Little, Brown & Co., 1970.

Mead, Margaret. *Male and Female: A Study of the Sexes in a Changing World.* New York: Laurel Editions, Dell Publishing Co., Inc., 1949.

Millar, J. D. "VD Control in the United States," *The Practicing Physician Confronts VD.* Proceedings of the Third International Venereal Disease Symposium, New Orleans, La., May 31–June 2, 1973. New York: Science and Medicine Publishing Co., Inc., 1974, pp. 19–21.

Miller, Jean Baker, Ed. *Psychoanalysis and Women.* Baltimore: Penguin Books, Inc., 1973.

Morgan, Robin, Ed. *Sisterhood Is Powerful: An Anthology of Writings from the Women's Liberation Movement.* New York: Vintage Books, Random House, 1970.

Mornell, Pierre. *The Lovebook.* New York: Harper & Row, 1974.

Moulton, Ruth. "A Survey and Reevaluation of the Concept of Penis Envy," *Psychoanalysis and Women.* Miller, Jean Baker, Ed. Baltimore: Penguin Books, Inc., 1973, pp. 239–58.

Nelson, Arvalea. "Personality Attributes of Female Orgasmic Consistency (or, Romance Makes You Frigid)," Unpublished M.A. Thesis for University of California, Berkeley, 1974.

Netter, Frank H. *The CIBA Collection of Medical Illustrations,* v. 2, Summit, New Jersey: CIBA Corporation, 1954, 1965.

Newton, Niles. "Interrelationships Between Sexual Responsiveness, Birth and Breast Feeding," *Contemporary Sexual Behavior: Critical Issues in the 1970's.* Zubin, Joseph and Money, John, Eds. American Psychopathological Association Proceedings, 61st, 1971. Baltimore: The Johns Hopkins University Press, 1973.

O'Connor, John F. and Stern, Lenore O. "Results of Treatment in Functional Sexual Disorders," *New York Journal of Medicine,* v. 72, no. 15, 1972, pp. 127–34.

Otto, Herbert A. and Otto, Roberta. *Total Sex.* New York: Signet, New American Library, 1972.

The Pearl. New York: Grove Press, 1967.

Pomeroy, Wardell. *Boys and Sex.* New York: Dell Publishing Co., Inc., 1968.

Pomeroy, Wardell. *Girls and Sex.* New York: Dell Publishing Co., Inc., 1969.

Pomeroy, Wardell. *Dr. Kinsey and the Institute for Sex Research.* New York: Signet, New American Library, 1973.

Pomeroy, Wardell. *Your Child and Sex: A Guide to Parents.* New York: Delacorte Press, 1974.

Reuben, David. *Everything You Always Wanted to Know About Sex* But Were Afraid to Ask.* New York: Bantam Books, National General Co., 1969.

Ribble, M. "The Infantile Experience in Relation to Personality Development," *Personality and the Behavior Disorders.* Hunt, J. McV., Ed. New York: Ronald Press, 1944, pp. 621–51.

Rogers, Carl R. *Becoming Partners: Marriage and Its Alternatives.* New York: Dell Publishing Co., Inc., 1972.

Rosenberg, Jack Lee. *Total Orgasm*. New York: Random House, and Berkeley: The Bookworks, 1973.

Rubin, I. "Sex After Forty—and After Seventy," *An Analysis of Human Sexual Response*. Brecher, Ruth and Brecher, Edward, Eds. New York: Signet, New American Library, 1966, pp. 251–66.

Rush, Ann Kent. *Getting Clear*. New York: Random House, and Berkeley: The Bookworks, 1973.

Schmidt, Gunter and Sigusch, Volkmar. "Women's Sexual Arousal," *Contemporary Sexual Behavior: Critical Issues in the 1970's*. Zubin, Joseph and Money, John, Eds. American Psychopathological Association Proceedings, 61st, 1971. Baltimore: The Johns Hopkins University Press, 1973.

Sherfey, Mary Jane. *The Nature and Evolution of Female Sexuality*. New York: Vintage Books, Random House, 1966, 1972.

Sherfey, Mary Jane. "On the Nature of Female Sexuality," *Psychoanalysis and Women*. Miller, Jean Baker, Ed. Baltimore: Penguin Books, Inc., 1973, pp. 135–54.

Sherfey, Mary Jane. "A Theory on Female Sexuality," *Sisterhood Is Powerful*. Morgan, Robin, Ed. New York: Vintage Books, Random House, 1970, pp. 220–29.

Shulman, Alix. "Organs and Orgasms," *Woman in Sexist Society*. Gornick, Vivian and Moran, Barbara K., Eds. New York: Signet, New American Library, 1971, pp. 292–303.

Solberg, Don A., Butler, Julius, and Wagner, Nathaniel N. "Sexual Behavior and Pregnancy," *The New England Journal of Medicine*, v. 288, no. 21, May 24, 1973, pp. 1098–1103.

Thompson, Clara M. *On Women*. New York: Mentor, New American Library, 1964, 1971.

Wallace, Doug and Barbach, Lonnie. "Pre-Orgasmic Group Treatment," *Journal of Sex and Marital Therapy*, v. 1, no. 2, 1975. In Press.

Wallach, Leah. "Vaginal vs. Clitoral Orgasm," *Forum*, v. 2, no. 7, September 1973, pp. 44–47.

Wallin, Paul and Clark, Alexander L. "A Study of Orgasm as a Condition of Woman's Enjoyment of Coitus in the Middle Years of Marriage," *Human Biology*, v. 35, May 1963, pp. 131–39.

Webster, New World Dictionary. College Edition. New York: The World Publishing Company, 1966.

Weisstein, Naomi. "Kinde, Kuche, Kirche As Scientific Law: Psychology Constructs the Female," *Sisterhood Is Powerful*. Morgan, Robin, Ed. New York: Vintage Books, Random House, 1970, pp. 205–19.

Young, Wayland. *Eros Denied*. New York: Grove Press, Inc., 1964.

Zubin, Joseph and Money, John, Eds. *Contemporary Sexual Behavior: Critical Issues in the 1970's*. American Psychopathological Association Proceedings, 61st, 1971. Baltimore: The Johns Hopkins University Press, 1973.

INDEX

Ovid, 29

Pain, 32
    in aging, 158
    in pregnancy, 152–53
Pairing, xiv
Pap smear, 161
PC muscle. *See* Pubococcygeal
        muscle
Pearl, The, 84
Penis, 23, 61 ff., 137. *See also*
        Intercourse; Oral sex
    children and, 33, 169
    size of, 22, 58
Perineum, 55
Petting, 92
"Plateaus," 104–06. *See also*
        Sexual response cycle
Playboy Foundation, ix, 25, 39,
        77, 92
    and oral sex, 148
    and positions, 150
Pomeroy, Wardell, 164
Pornography, 76 ff., 82–85, 98–
        99
Positions, 150. *See also* Inter-
        course; specific positions
Potts, Leah, 47, 64
Pregnancy and childbirth, 59,
        152–53, 159
Premarital sex, 38 ff., 88
Premature ejaculation, 172
Preoccupation, 75
Prepuce (clitoral hood), 55, 57,
        62, 63, 66
    in sexological exercise, 137
Progesterone, 158
Puberty (adolescence), 37 ff.,
        166–67
    rites, 36–37
Pubococcygeal muscle (PC mus-
        cle), 59–61, 66, 67, 73. *See
        also* Kegel exercises
    in sexological exercise, 59
Pulse rate, 66, 67

Radical Sex Manual, 149
Rape, 24
    fantasies, 80–81

Rappelling, 105
Rear entry position, 150, 155
Religion, 32, 62
    and masturbation, 91
Reuben, David, x, 70–71, 148
Rock climbing, 105–06
Rogers, Carl, xiv
Role-playing, 107
Roles, changing, 147
Rosenberg, on mutual mastur-
        bation, 138

Sado-masochism fantasies, 81
Saliva, 65, 96, 148
Schmidt and Sigusch, 77
Screaming, 25. *See also* Noise
Scrotum, 137
Seduction fantasies, 80, 81
Self Love, 90
Sensuous Woman, 48–49
"Sex flush," 66
Sex Information and Education
        Council of the United
        States, 154
*Sexual Behavior in the Human
        Female,* 69
Sexual Behavior in the 1970's.
        See Hunt, Morton
Sexual response cycle, 64–69
Sherfey, Mary Jane, 69, 89
Shulman, Alix, 41, 151, 169
Side by side position, 150
SIECUS, 154
Simultaneous orgasm, 117–18
Sitting position, 150
Smegma, 63
Soap, 73
Solberg, Butler, and Wagner,
        152 ff.
Sounds. *See* Noises
Spanking fantasies, 81
Spontaneous orgasm, 63
Surgery, vaginal, 17
Syphilis, 160

T'ai Chi, 103
Talking with partner, 125–26 ff.
Tampons, 36